Matthew W

Colour profiles
Kjetil Åkra

Blackburn
Skua & Roc

STRATUS

Published in Poland in 2007
by STRATUS s.c.
P.O. Box 123,
27-600 Sandomierz 1, Poland
e-mail: office@mmpbooks.biz
for
Mushroom Model Publications,
36 Ver Road, Redbourn,
AL3 7PE, UK.
e-mail: rogerw@mmpbooks.biz
© 2007 Mushroom Model
Publications.
http://www.mmpbooks.biz

All rights reserved. Apart from any fair dealing for the purpose of private study, research, criticism or review, as permitted under the Copyright, Design and Patents Act, 1988, no part of this publication may be reproduced, stored in a retrieval system, or transmitted in any form or by any means, electronic, electrical, chemical, mechanical, optical, photocopying, recording or otherwise, without prior written permission. All enquiries should be addressed to the publisher.

ISBN
978-83-89450-44-9

Editor in chief
Roger Wallsgrove

Editorial Team
Bartłomiej Belcarz
Artur Juszczak
James Kightly
Robert Pęczkowski

Colour Drawings
Kjetil Åkra

Scale plans
Dariusz Karnas

DTP
Robert Pęczkowski
Artur Juszczak

Printed by:
Drukarnia Diecezjalna,
ul. Żeromskiego 4,
27-600 Sandomierz
tel. +48 (15) 832 31 92;
fax +48 (15) 832 77 87
www.wds.pl marketing@wds.pl

PRINTED IN POLAND

Contents

Acknowledgements 3
Foreword by Lieutenant-Commander Derek Martin 4
Introduction 6
Background and Development 8
Blackburn Roc 23
The 'Pit Ponies' 32
Norway 44
Dunkirk and the Channel 69
Return to Norway… 76
The Mediterranean 81
The end 92
Second line duties 95
Future developments 102
The Skua and Roc Described 105
Conclusion 112
Detail photos 114
    Fuselage & Engine 114
    Cockpit & Canopy 122
    Wing 125
    Undercarriage 126
Colour Photos 129
Colour profiles 142

Get in the picture!
Do you have photographs of historical aircraft, airfields in action, or original and unusual stories to tell?
MMP would like to hear from you! We welcome previously unpublished material that will help to make MMP books the best of their kind. We will return original photos to you and provide full credit for your images. Contact us before sending us any valuable material: rogerw@mmpbooks.biz

On the title page: Five Rocs in formation, August 1940. The flat underside of the Roc, lacking the bomb recess of the Skua, can be seen. (Central Press Photographs, courtesy of BAE Systems Brough Heritage)

Acknowledgements

Behind the writing of this book lies the unstinting and freely given support of a very large number of people without whom this volume would never have happened. These include ex-servicemen who agreed to discuss their experiences of the Skua and Roc with me – Derek Martin, Cecil Filmer, Ron Jordan, Lloyd Richards, Derrick Edwards, Eric Brown; the relatives of Skua and Roc crews who provided selfless support and shared memoirs, documents and correspondence with me – Simon Partridge, Denis Rolph, Ron Campbell; The associations and organisations, and individuals therein that have provided reams of information along with support and assistance. These are the Fleet Air Arm Museum, in particular Catherine Rounsfell and Jan Keohane of the Research Department, and Dave Morris and Graham Mottram; The Norsk Luftfartmuseum, in particular Birger Larsen and Klas Gjølmesli; The National Archives, in particular the staff from the Records Copying Department; The Orkney Archive, in particular Gary Amos and Alison Fraser; BAE Systems Brough Heritage Department (whose photographic library is astonishing) particularly Steve Gillard; The Aviation Bookshop, who sought out rare volumes and arranged a meeting with Captain Eric 'Winkle' Brown; The Telegraphist Air Gunners (TAGs) Association, in particular Ken Davies. There are a number of individuals who have made invaluable contributions. Lieutenant Commander Martin very kindly provided a foreword from the perspective of one who took a Skua into battle; Øyvind Lamo, (who started the Skua renaissance by discovering the wreckage of Captain Partridge's L2940 on the bed of Lake Grotli) and Captain Partridge's son, Simon, have untiringly put me in touch with more people and information than I can describe – to Øyvind and to Simon gratitude is also due for inviting me to the reunion of Skua aircrew at the Fleet Air Arm Museum on October 29th 2006. A third vote of thanks goes to Simon who assisted with the research on the fateful raid on the Scharnhorst in June 1940. John Dell, who runs an excellent Skua website, provided photographs, contacts and invaluable information, while Peter C. Smith has published more than any everyone else put together on the Skua and without the information already unearthed by John and Peter this book could not have happened. Steven Jefferson and Pat Chilton kindly arranged access to Pat's father's photo library and some of Captain Chilton's fantastic images can be found within. There are also those who contributed directly to the book you see before you – illustrator Kjetil Åkra who has the patience of a saint and the eye of an artist, Ian Huntley who drew from his immense knowledge to advise on the drawings and whose published information was invaluable to the colour information, and of course editors James Kightly and Roger Wallsgrove, who generously agreed to the project and tempered the text into the finished article. Last but very far from least, my wife Ros whose support was immeasurable.

Foreword by Lieutenant-Commander Derek Martin

When the author asked me to consider writing a foreword he was granting me a very dubious honour since my operational experience in the Skua when in 800 Squadron was abruptly terminated on the 13th of June 1940 over Trondheim when partaking in a futile gesture of revenge following the sinking of HMS *Glorious* and her two escorts, *Ardent* and *Acasta*, on the 8th of June. However, as I appear in the text I felt honour bound – dubious or not – to agree.

It has not proved very easy, evoking as it did distant and long forgotten memories of 66 years ago: some exciting, some frightening and, even more alarming, my inability to recall some vital details at all. The return course to steer for *Ark Royal* for example: in the event this choice was removed. But I digress.

I completed the fighter course at HMS *Raven*, near Southampton, early in 1940. Skuas were the aircraft mainly used and much attention was paid to Aerodrome Dummy Deck Landings (ADDLs) – i.e. touching down on a 20ft circle in the middle of the airfield. We had a few Gladiators reserved largely for the CO to test close formation flying at 'zero' feet over Salisbury Plain. There followed live deck landings.

The Skua was to the Fleet Air Arm what the Spitfire was to the RAF though its performance was in no way comparable. But this did not matter – it was the first fighter in the Royal Navy worthy of the name – and if not 'tailor made' it had at least been 'tailor modified' to suit naval air requirements. This included the essential capability of carrying a second crew member thus allowing the facility of a trained Observer or Telegraphist Air Gunner to navigate the aircraft to its carrier over hundreds of square miles of a featureless sea. The description given in the book suggests its pre-production problems were resolved by an 'ad hoc' process – a committee design. It had its shortcomings – underpowered, not very comfortable, not very suitable for aerobatics and highly dangerous in a spin which required the afterthought of a tail parachute.: an aeroplane which needed sensible handling in the air. It was however strongly built and entirely suitable for dive-bombing with its very strong air brakes; it was very easy to deck land with its excellent visibility and quite capable of coping with a heavy deck landing, sometimes unavoidable if the ship was pitching too much. It had a good range – four and a half hours safe maximum and a very reliable sleeve-valve engine. Not all pilots liked it, but most did; we all however envied the Spitfire.

The operational life of the Skua was relatively short and, as the author points out was withdrawn from frontline service after the Norwegian campaign ended.

It continued to be of use in several secondary functions and has made its mark in naval aviation much as the Swordfish did. As far as I'm aware no other naval aircraft designed and built in Great Britain as a fighter for the Royal Navy has generated so much interest – and as a dive bomber it had great potential and achieved some notable success in its short history. I cannot testify to its dive bombing record because I never did any: I can, however testify that it was useless against Me109s – even one.

Mr. Willis's book is not a book of reference and is more enjoyable to read for that reason and deserves a place in the records of our naval aviation. I hope it will sustain the memory of this rather unique aircraft which the Fleet Air Arm Museum at Yeovilton is doing since it put on display the remains of a Skua salvaged after thirty years submerged in Norwegian fjord. This dedicated team of Norwegians continued a relentless search for Skua remains scattered over large areas of the country and have amassed a considerable quantity of material with which they are determined will allow them to reconstitute a complete cockpit and are I believe within 75% of achieving their end target. Visit the Yeovilton Museum, and if possible, the Norwegian equivalent at Bodø and enjoy this book.

DTR Martin, No. 5 Pilots' Course, March 1939,
HMS Frobisher, Portsmouth

When it was introduced the Skua was promoted as the epitome of speed and modernity though in reality it was virtually obsolescent by the time it entered service. This advertisement is from a programme for the 1938 Hendon air display.

Introduction

The Blackburn Skua is an aircraft of contradictions and one which polarised opinions even before it entered production. The views of those who flew it ranged from high praise to a damning indictment; from 'first class' and 'one of the best' to 'too heavy, too slow, too late'.

The Skua was a two seat fighter and dive bomber developed for naval use following a specification issued by the Air Ministry in 1934. The Roc was a development of the Skua equipped with a power-operated turret in the manner of the Boulton Paul Defiant.

The modern perceptions of the Skua and Roc are of aircraft thrown into a war they were ill-equipped to fight, emblematic of the second-rate equipment foisted on the Fleet Air Arm (FAA) in the first days of the war and with which the naval aircrews merely muddled through. The Skua and Roc seem to share none of the character of that loveable, ludicrous old warhorse the Swordfish, and precious little of the glory. There are many notable achievements in the work of the Skua, and even the Roc, but most are still unsung.

The Skua equipped four front-line FAA squadrons between August 1938 and May 1941. The Roc equipped no squadrons exclusively but operated alongside Skuas in small numbers. The majority of the action in the Skua's service career came during the ultimately unsuccessful attempts to prevent the Germans overrunning Norway in 1940, beginning with the sinking of the cruiser *Königsberg* in Bergen harbour, the first destruction of a large warship by aircraft in the war. The Roc, meanwhile, is perhaps best known for its operations during the evacuation of Allied forces at Dunkirk.

Perhaps it is the nature of these campaigns, bravely fought but redolent of failure, which have influenced perceptions of the aircraft. It would be easy to categorise the Skua and Roc with the Douglas TBD-1 Devastator or the Caudron-Renault 714 – hopelessly inadequate aircraft hurled at a superior enemy, chiefly notable for the courage of aircrews who willingly undertook their duty faced with the very real possibility of destruction. The Air Ministry wanted the Skua and Roc cancelled, while the Naval Staff seemed eager to hasten replacement by aircraft with barely superior performance. This has never helped the Skua's reputation, but many in the FAA felt that its passing was premature and subsequently mourned the lack of an effective dive bomber for the next three years of the war. The Skua, like the Swordfish, even earned itself a nickname born of equal parts affection and deprecation – the 'Screwball'.

Both aircraft had their failings, and not insignificant ones at that. It would be difficult to argue that the Roc was anything other than a failure if only because the tactical doctrines which led to its design were fatally flawed. The Skua was unquestionably too slow for a fighter. Nevertheless the latter at least would prove itself to be a powerful weapon and showed what might have been possible had the Fleet Air Arm been able to use it differently. Both Skua and Roc served out the war in unglamorous but useful duties as trainers and target tugs - a poor use for the Navy's best dive bomber.

Recently there has been a resurgence of interest in the Skua. In Norway, divers discovered the wreckage of aircraft lost during the attempt to stem the German invasion, and museums began collecting the components that still litter the hillsides around former battlegrounds. Thanks to the efforts of those such as Øyvind Lamo, who discovered Captain Partridge's L2940 near Grotli, and the team from the Norsk Luftfartmuseum at Bodo, there is for the first time since 1945, the possibility of a complete Skua – and the reality of a rebuilt cockpit section. The Norwegians have taken the Skua to their hearts as a symbol of the alliance between Britain and Norway in 1940, and were it not for their determination, the Skua would be nothing but a memory. The crowning glory of this priceless work is the discovery on the 25th April 2007 of a virtually complete Skua lying on the bed of Trondheimfjord by a team led by Martin Ludvigsen and Klas Gjølmesli using a search vessel, the MV *Gunnerus* provided by Norwegian University of Science and Technology. The Skua was that flown by Lieutenant Commander John Casson during the disastrous raid on the *Scharnhorst* in June 1940. It has lain forgotten and undisturbed for 67 years, but plans to raise the wreck may soon mean that the Blackburn Skua is no longer an effectively extinct species.

Prototype K5178 under construction at Blackburn's Brough factory. The spaceframe engine attachment at the firewall is shorter than on production models and the powerplant is a Bristol Mercury. Note the oil tank ahead of the cockpit – the upper surface of the tank forms part of the aircraft's skin. (BAE Systems)

Background and Development

The Skua story starts long before G.E. Petty and his team at Blackburn began to consider a response to Air Ministry specification O.27/34. Some examination of the state of the Fleet Air Arm between the wars is necessary to understand how the Skua came into being.

The Admiralty was based around the same basic structure as at the beginning of the First World War, and was still struggling to come to terms with naval aviation, in terms of materiel and operation. The Naval Aviation Department (NAD) contained most of the officers with direct experience of naval aviation in the Admiralty, and reported to 'their Lordships' – the First Lord of the Admiralty (a cabinet post and civilian minister), and the five Sea Lords who were professional RN officers. The 1st Sea Lord had overall day-to-day responsibility for the running of the RN, while the 5th Sea Lord was in charge of the new Air Branch. However, until the Fleet Air Arm was handed back to the RN in 1937, the RAF still had responsibility for equipment and men. This structure caused numerous problems for the Fleet Air Arm, as those with direct knowledge of naval air matters could be overruled or circumvented by those without. Before the naval air matters were fully handed over to the navy, conflicts of interest between the Air Staff, RAF and RN could take place all too easily and the requirement for a new naval strike fighter in 1934 was no exception...

In 1930, officers of the new aircraft carrier HMS *Courageous* wrote a paper promoting the idea of multi-role aircraft for the Navy. The FAA's limited resources meant limited numbers of aircraft. Incorporating several roles in each aircraft meant the maximum could be extracted from each airframe, aircrew and square foot of deck and hanger space and made the whole air group a more flexible force. There was some practical corroboration throughout the 1930s for this theory. It led to some highly successful aircraft such as the Hawker Osprey, which performed only slightly less well than single seat fighters, had a second crew member for navigation over the sea, and could carry a small bomb load.

The apogee of the multi-role naval aircraft was Fairey's Torpedo-Spotter-Reconnaissance (TSR), the Swordfish. Dated on its introduction and an anachronism at the beginning of the war, it was so versatile and well-liked by aircrew that, with the Osprey, it set the pattern for British naval aircraft. These two aircraft persuaded the Navy that all necessary functions could be fulfilled in two types of aircraft, the TSR and strike-fighter. If any new capabilities were to be added to the Fleet Air Arm repertoire, they would have to be shoehorned into one of these categories.

During November 1934 the Ministry discussed with the Navy the required dimensions, function and performance of the aircraft that was intended to bring the Fleet Air Arm into the modern era.

The naval representatives lobbied for the new aircraft to be able to dive-bomb. They were impressed with the development of naval dive-bombing in the US, and had built a mock section of a battleship at Chatham to explore

The first Skua prototype K5178, photographed in flight between February and June 1937 (when the fuselage gained a large '8' as identification for the Hendon air display that year). The differences from the production Skua can be clearly seen – notably the lack of upswept wingtips, the shorter nose and bulges on the cowling to accommodate the Bristol Mercury radial. (BAE Systems)

the effects of different types of bombing on ships at sea. They were convinced that dive-bombing offered considerable potential. Fairey Flycatcher and Hawker Osprey flights had therefore trained in light dive bombing with small bomb racks beneath their wings, but the Navy now wanted a dedicated, heavy dive bomber capable of crippling or destroying ships at sea. The Air Ministry's historical indifference to dive bombing seemed finally to have been overcome, though the Navy never received the dive-bombing sight they had been asking for since the early 1930s.

The role of naval fighter was itself more complex than that of a land based fighter. It involved escorting strike aircraft to and from the target, undertaking standing patrols and reconnaissance as well as some strike missions itself. The RN's belief that a pilot could not navigate the required distances on his own effectively sealed the two-seat layout for the new aircraft. The RAF broadly settled on the straightforward interceptor and later added other functions while the RN needed the full range of options in one machine.

The Admiralty still believed that naval fighters would not be likely to encounter land-based fighters, so versatility was more important than outright performance. This gives some context to the preference the Navy expressed in the specification meetings for dive bombing to be the first requirement of O.27/34.

Essentially, the Navy recognised that a specialised design was needed to dive bomb well, but thought that the compromises to fighter performance that dive bombing capability would necessitate would be acceptable. Aircraft that are stressed for dive bombing are typically 20% heavier than they would otherwise need to be, and this would clearly affect the aircraft's overall performance.

The dive-bomber fighter would therefore have two aircrew, and able 'to disable the opposing fleet air arm by dive bombing attacks on hostile carriers and... to engage hostile aircraft in the air'[1] (in that order). It was to be not greater than 33ft in length, with a wingspan of 46ft and a width with wings folded of not more than 16ft.

On the 12th of December the Air Ministry invited Vickers, Blackburn and Avro to submit designs for a Hawker Osprey replacement. An existing design by A.V. Roe was allowed to be submitted. This was the Type 666, a biplane powered by an Armstrong-Siddeley Tiger, with enclosed cockpit and fixed, single-strut undercarriage.

Two months later Blackburn tendered the B-24, a low-wing monoplane of all-metal construction. Vickers also participated with the Type 280, a mid-wing monoplane with semi-elliptical mainplanes, powered by a Rolls-Royce Merlin.[2] Vickers' design appeared to highly thought-of by the Air Ministry but had run into trouble by the beginning of 1936. The RAE felt that the only way to improve severe spin recovery problems that model tests had revealed would be to lengthen the tail by three feet, and design work stopped while this was resolved. The increase in length caused the Vickers design to exceed the specified dimensions, so the specification was amended to increase length by 3ft to give all the manufacturers the same concession.

On the 11th February the Director of Technical Development (DTD) wrote to the company to emphasise 'the importance of not letting up on this type', and requested 'the full co-operation of Vickers in proceeding with the design to the best of their ability'.[3] Nevertheless, it seems the problems could not be

It is unclear exactly what colours Skua prototype K5178 wore in early 1937 – the fuselage may have been pale green, blue or grey while the wings and tail surfaces were probably silver but may have been white. The wing undersides are the same colour as the fuselage, while Type A roundels were worn on the fuselage and upper and lower wing surfaces. (BAE Systems)

Skua fuselage in a substantial jig at Blackburn in May 1938, possibly for structural testing. (BAE Systems)

overcome, as just over a month later, the Air Ministry decided to order 150 of the Blackburn design, and the company was instructed to build two prototypes.

On the 24th October 1936, the Air Ministry confirmed the production contract for Blackburn B-24s, adding a further forty aircraft which brought the total production to 190. Specification 25/36 requested the Blackburn to be produced with a number of modifications to the original design. This included replacement of the Bristol Mercury radial fitted to the prototypes with a 9-cylinder Bristol Perseus PRE3M. This was the first production sleeve valve design by Bristol and was intended to provide a leap in performance over the traditional poppet-valve engine. Sleeve valves replaced the normal reciprocating valve with a tube rotating about the cylinder running off gears. The system theoretically offers greater simplicity, reduced mechanical losses and greater reliability, though the new design needed considerable work before it could equal the best poppet-

Second prototype (Skua MkI) K5179 nearing completion at the Blackburn factory in February 1938. The aircraft flew in May that year. The Alclad structure of the unpainted airframe is very much in evidence. The second prototype had a longer nose than the earlier aircraft, but shared with K5178 Bristol Mercury power and the 'MkI' cowling, which is longer and less tapered than the Perseus cowling. Note the different oil cooler intake under the cowling, further forward than Perseus engined aircraft. (BAE Systems)

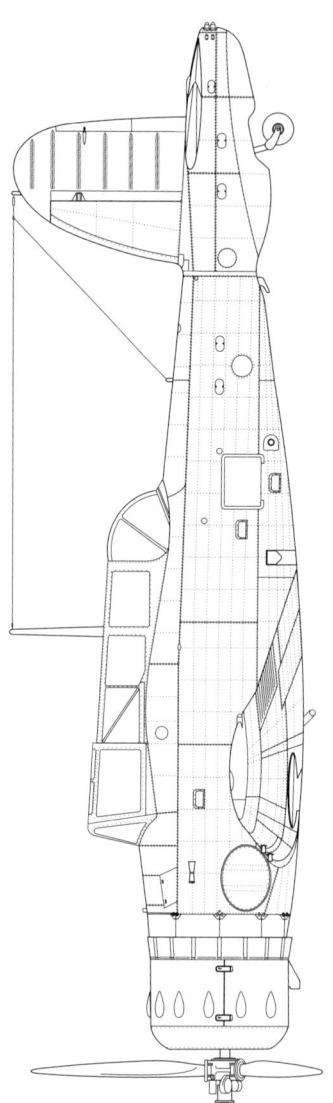

Blackburn Skua first prototype.
1/72 scale.

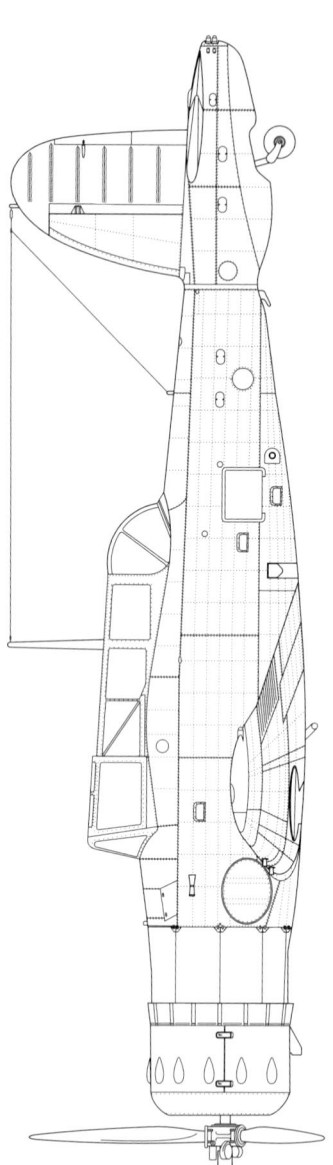

Blackburn Skua second prototype.
1/72 scale.

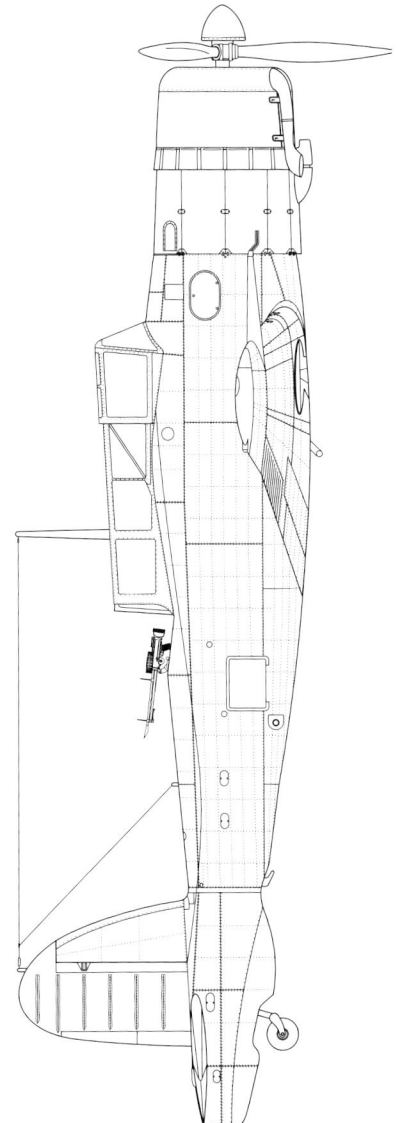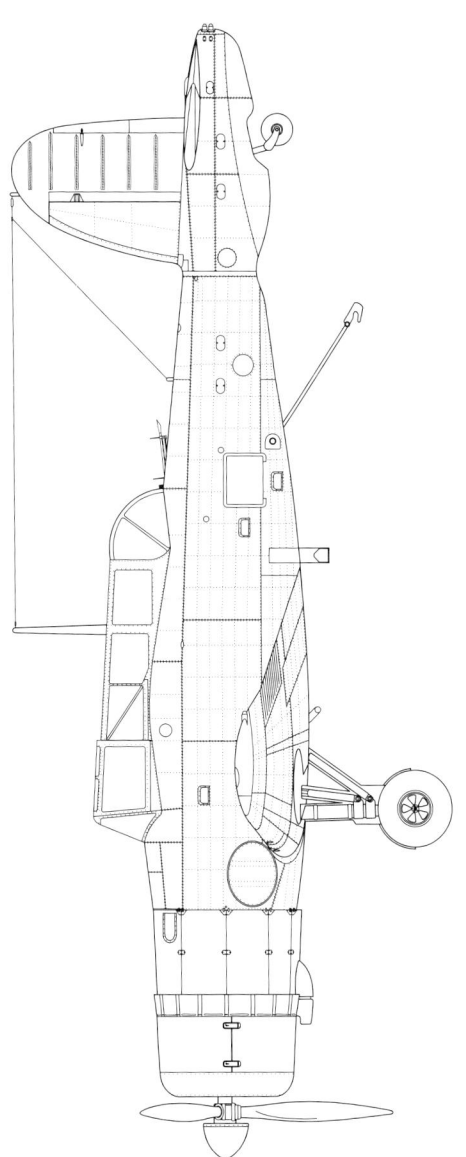

*Blackburn Skua.
1/72 scale.*

Production Skua under construction. The longer nose and engine mount (which has gained a 'bay' over the prototype) of the production Skua MkII, and differences in the cylinder heads of the sleeve-valve Bristol Perseus over the poppet-valve Mercury fitted to K5178 can be clearly seen when compared with photographs of the prototype. Note the substantial exhaust exiting from a collector ring in the front of the cowling. (BAE Systems)

valve designs for power and reliability. The order also specified four Browning .303in machine guns in the wings with 600 rounds per gun, and a Lewis Mk III machine gun in the rear cockpit. At this stage the largest bomb to be carried was a 250lb general purpose device. The Air Ministry also requested that the aircraft could be readily converted for target towing.

Following successful model tests by the RAE the B-24 prototype K5178 took to the air for the first time at the hands of Blackburn's chief test pilot, Captain A.M. 'Dasher' Blake, on 9th February 1937. The public got its first

L2870 following a landing accident aboard HMS Courageous before the outbreak of war, damaging the undercarriage and port flap - the arrestor hook is intact suggesting the pilot missed the wires. This Skua, one of the early production machines, was employed in carrier landing trials in 1938 and 1939. (Author's collection)

view of the new aircraft at the Hendon RAF display on the 26th June 1937, when K5178 was displayed in New Types Park. On the 17th August the name 'Skua' was officially assigned to the type by the Air Ministry, this being a sea bird that dives from height to catch its food.

In November Blackburn delivered K5178 to the Aeroplane and Armament Evaluation Establishment (A&AEE) at Martlesham Heath for handling trials, which were completed with generally favourable results. The cockpit's layout and forward view drew praise from the test pilots and handling was found to be generally acceptable, although there were some issues with stability and stall characteristics. The Skua had a tendency to nose up into a stall by itself if the controls were released, and stability in all planes was poor below 140 knots. Though the stall was not vicious it could, if uncorrected, lead to a wing drop and spin.

Following the initial handling trials, to assess the Skua's suitability for dive-bombing the terrifying-sounding 'terminal velocity' tests were employed, wherein the aircraft was put into a vertical dive from 20,000 feet until drag equalled the downward force of the plummeting aircraft. Fortunately for the test pilots, the Skua had a relatively low terminal velocity for a monoplane of no more than 280 knots, thanks in no small part to its effective flaps.

K5178 was fitted with upturned wingtips during testing in 1937 to improve lateral stability. This modification was easy to incorporate as the Skua featured detachable wingtips. It had a similar effect to increasing the dihedral, but without Blackburn being required to alter the production tooling dramatically. The Roc was able to take better advantage of this with an increased dihedral angle, and was indeed found to have greater stability than the Skua.

A spring tensioner was attached to the elevator controls in a further attempt to reduce the longitudinal instability at low speeds. This was only effective when the power was off and the aircraft was travelling slowly, leading the RAE to suspect that the problem was caused by the wash of the propeller affecting the airflow over the tail surfaces.

In December 1937 and January 1938 the RAE tested K5178 with a number of aerodynamic devices designed to improve the stall characteristics. These included a spoiler on

One of the early production Skuas during the trial programme in 1938-9. The aircraft has not been fitted with a bomb crutch. The complex underside shape of the Skua is apparent, with triangular-section 'fillets' joining the wing to the round-section fuselage. (via John Dell)

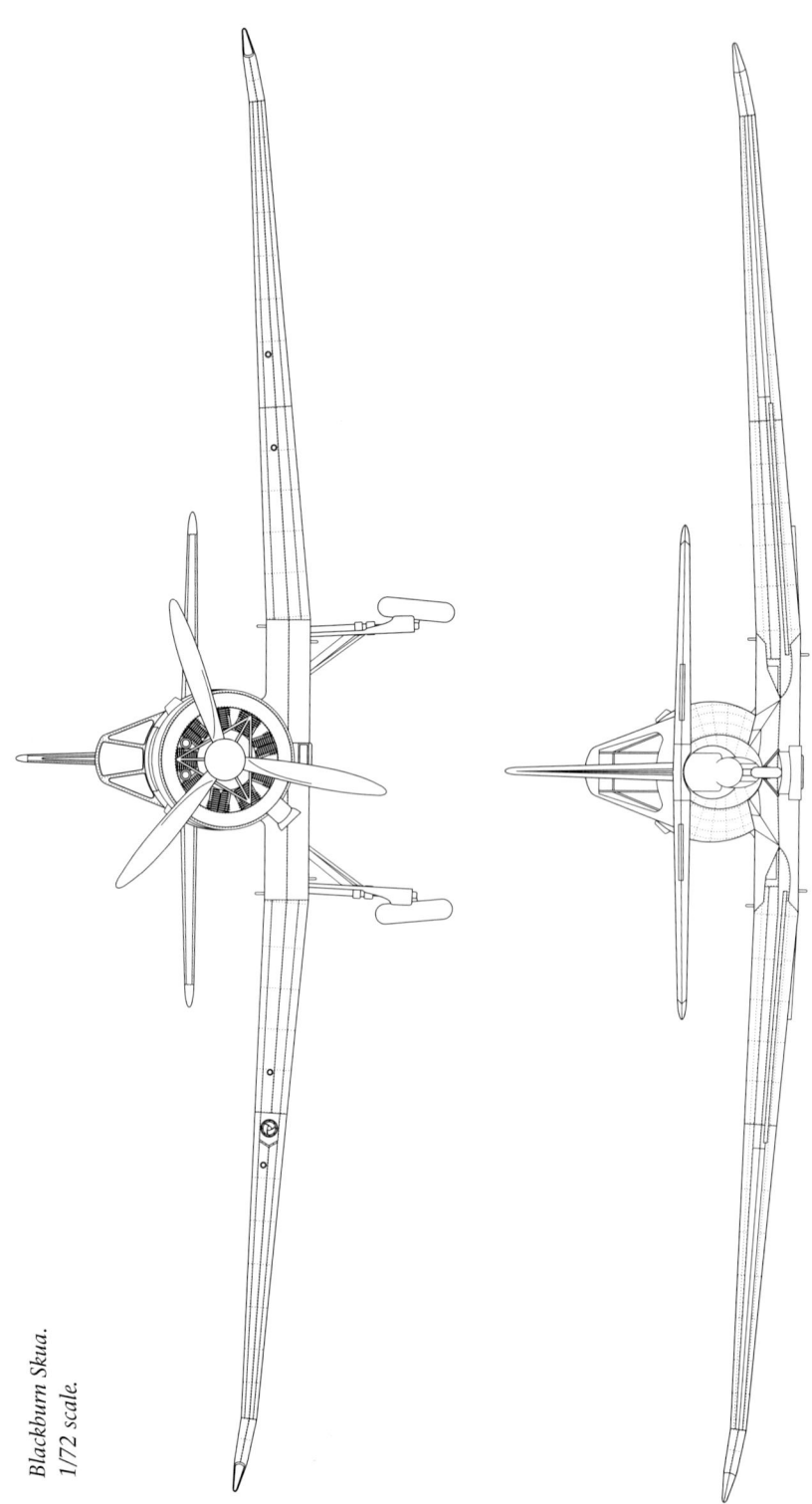

*Blackburn Skua.
1/72 scale.*

Skua production in full swing in July 1939. There are seventeen Skuas awaiting completion in the photograph, and a solitary Botha torpedo bomber in the background. The aircraft in the centre is painted in the black and yellow stripes denoting target-tug use, while the rest appear to be silver doped or unpainted. Different panels vary distinctly in tone. (BAE Systems)

the upper wing surface near the root and pointed fairings of various sizes on the leading edge near the root. These were intended to allow the inner wing to stall slightly earlier than the outer wing, therefore giving the pilot some warning before the wing dropped. The spoilers and LE extensions made the stall occur more gradually and gave more warning before deep turbulence covered the wing leading to a sudden loss of lift but also raised the stalling speed by some 4 knots and were therefore not proceeded with.[4]

As a result of these tests and other experiences from the wind tunnel, the tail plane gained longer, rounded tips intended to protrude outside the prop-wash and increase stability. Leading-edge slats were recommended, as was an interim anti-stall parachute, a jury-rigged affair triggered by a chord led externally from the cockpit to the tail and held in place by strips of doped fabric. The watertight compartments in the fuselage sadly prevented a more elegant solution short of a major redesign.

Blackburn were able to take advantage of some of the lessons learned with the testing of K5178 with the second prototype, K5179 which first flew on the 4th of May 1938. The nose was lengthened by 2' 4¾" to try to cure the self-stall and the upturned wingtips as retro-fitted to K5178 were included. Leading edge slots as recommended by the RAE were fitted too, though these did not show any improvement and were omitted from production aircraft. It was later found that the most probable cause of the longitudinal instability was the height of the centre of gravity above the wing chord.

Second prototype K5179 replaced K5178 for handling trials at the A&AEE while the original machine was retained for armament trials. Through a proc-

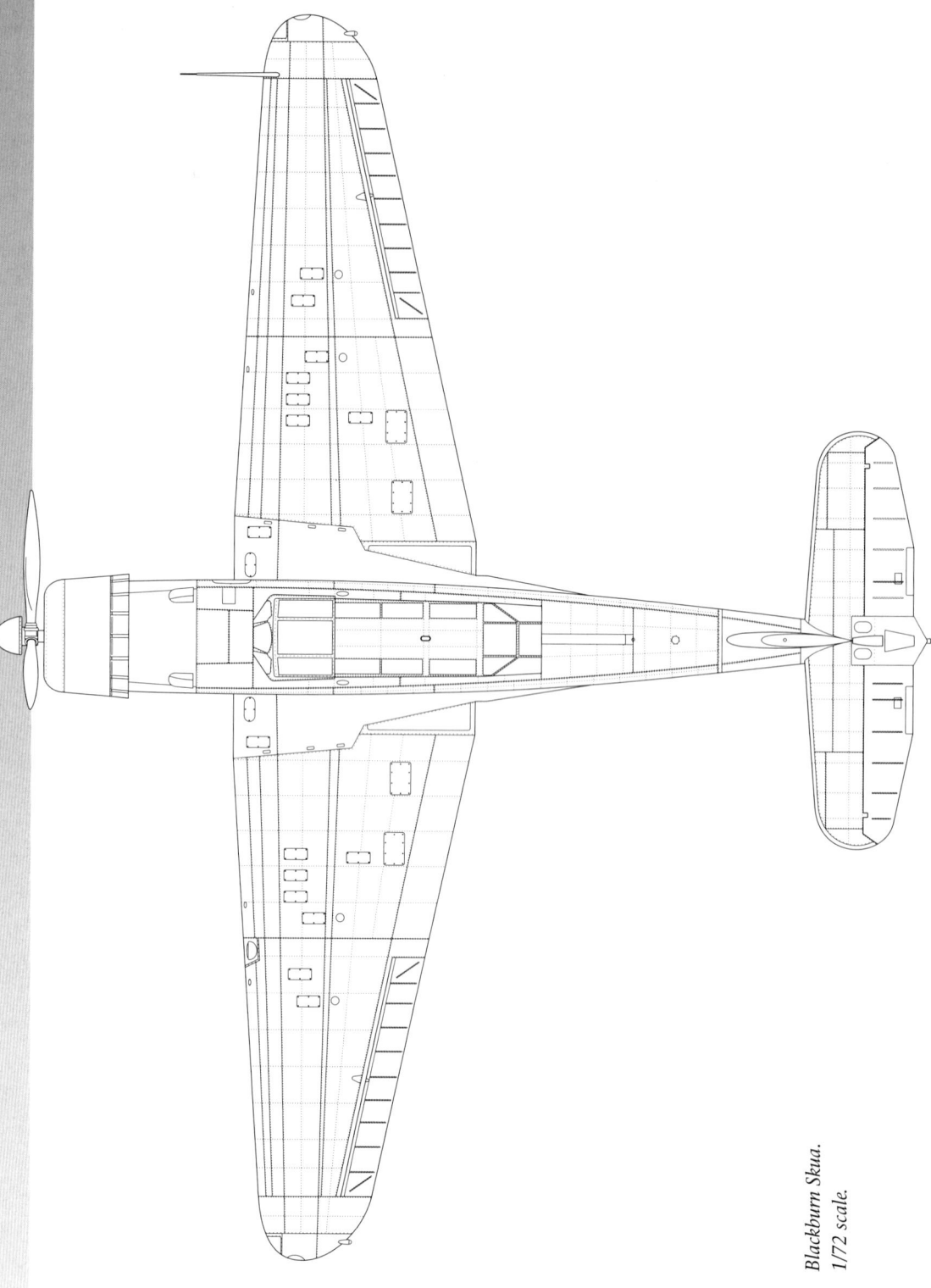

*Blackburn Skua.
1/72 scale.*

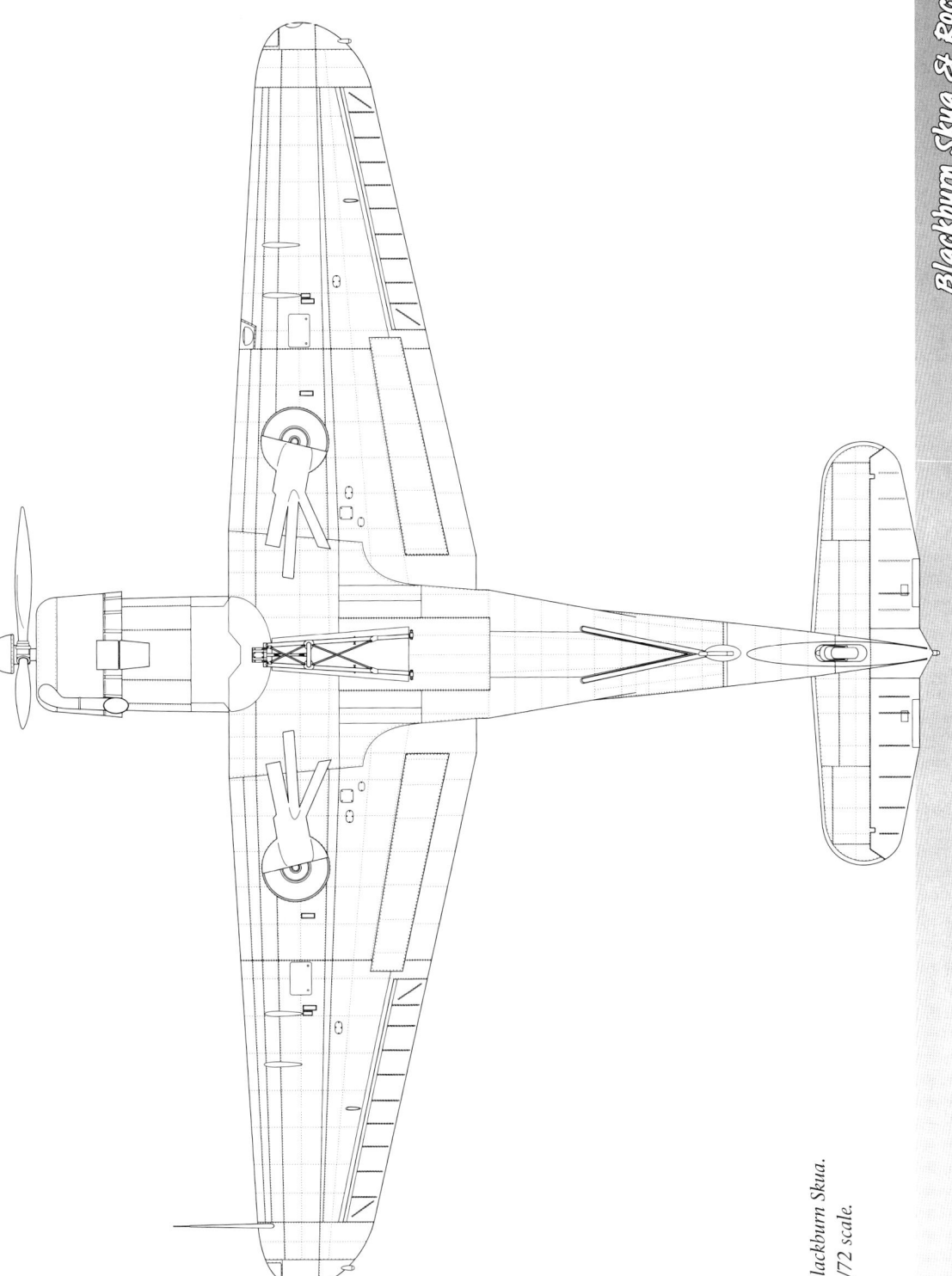

Blackburn Skua. 1/72 scale.

Blackburn Skua & Roc

ess of testing, modification and trial, many of the negative characteristics had been cured or reduced. The slats had not made much difference, so the 'interim' anti-spin parachute was retained, and the RAE recommended that aerobatics were prohibited below 5,000ft. The spinning issues were never entirely resolved as Petty Officer Harold Arthur 'Eric' Monk recounts: 'It is... true the Skua was loath to recover from a spin and one of 800 Squadron's Skuas recovered from a spin only to promptly spin the other way and dive into the Forth'.[5]

In May 1938, the first two production machines, L2867 and L2868, were delivered to the A&AEE after contractor's trials at Brough. These were to the final Mk II standard, except for L2867 which lacked the new klaxon to warn the pilot in the event of a wheels-up landing (a bell, as fitted to the prototypes, had proved inaudible at times) but included a number of extra instruments to help with testing. The two new aircraft were found to have improved directional stability, and pitch stability had been enhanced somewhat by the extended tail planes and the elevator spring tensioner. With these modifications, the lengthened nose and the upturned wingtips, the handling of the Skua was felt to be acceptable for service use. A few modifications had still to be made; a different oil pump was fitted following a series of engine failures. There was also a spate of structural failures in the connection between the detachable rear fuselage and the main body, which entailed returning the rear fuselages to Brough. A number of tails had to be returned from *Ark Royal* on cruise and had to be

A production scene shows two Skuas in full 'wasp stripe' target tug scheme, as pioneered by L3007 and subsequently adopted for all target towing aircraft. One is L2987 while the other is not identifiable. L2987 was the first target tug to be delivered - it went to No.5 Maintenance Unit at Kemble in July 1939 and transferred to the Admiralty. (BAE Systems)

done hurriedly as Blackburn were about to scrap the jigs and toolings, suggesting that barely more than a year after production began, the FAA did not want any more Skuas. (The Skua never entirely lost its reputation for losing its tail under some circumstances). One final modification was made out of expediency. The Navy had removed the arrestor hooks from all its retired Blackburn Sharks, so Blackburn were instructed to fit these surplus hooks to Skuas and Rocs as the design was very similar.

There was another hurdle for Blackburn before the aircraft was to enter service; in June 1938, three months before the Skua was due to enter service, the new Air Materiel Department of the Air Ministry recommended that the aircraft be cancelled on the basis that it was approaching obsolescence as a fighter. The Naval Air Department resisted as there was nothing to replace it with (even the stop-gap Fairey Fulmar would not be ready until the middle of 1940), and cancellation would leave the Navy with no dive bomber for the foreseeable future.

In September of 1938, the Skua entered service. Blackburn indicated that delivery of the 190 airframes would be completed by March 1940, considerably later than originally intended.

With the threat of cancellation over, the Skua continued its test programme. Production machine L2870 was used for deck landing trials, while L2867 was sent to the Royal Aircraft Establishment to clear the Skua for 'accelerator' use, target-towing and to test the radio equipment. The Blackburn passed the catapult trials with flying colours; the RAE assessment noted '...no criticisms. In fact, this aircraft is the first one which was designed around the catapult spools and not the spools attached to the aircraft afterwards'.[6] Thus cleared, L2867 proceeded to join HMS *Courageous* for accelerator tests at sea. Meanwhile, the first prototype K5178 went to HMS Pegasus for ditching trials at the end of January.

In February 1939, the Director of Technical Development (DTD) asked Blackburn to consider ways of allowing the 500lb Semi Armour Piercing (SAP) bomb to be carried, following discussions arising from the deck trials on Courageous. This would become the Skua's chief weapon as a dive bomber, though it was still comparatively small as a main weapon next to those of contemporary dive bombers.

1   Air Ministry Specification O.27/34
2   See K J Meekcoms and E B Morgan, The British Aircraft Specifications File, pp.198-199
3   Documents from the National Archives under AVIA 46/144
4   Francis and Pringle, Notes on the Flight Tests of the Blackburn Skua Prototype, RAE May 1938, National Archives under AVIA 6/2220
5   Letter from H A Monk to Ron Campbell 18th September 2001, reproduced by kind permission of Mr. Campbell
6   Francis and Pringle, Notes on the Flight Tests of the Blackburn Skua Prototype, RAE May 1938, National Archives under AVIA 6/2220

Blackburn Roc camouflage patterns. Not to scale.

Blackburn Roc

Specification O.30/35 for a naval turret fighter was issued directly to Blackburn on 31st December 1935. Blackburn had been working on a turret-fighter for some time, apparently with both the Navy and the RAF in mind*. The Navy had been influenced by the Air Ministry's enthusiasm for this type of aircraft.

The concept of the turret fighter, of which the Roc was the first to enter service, derived from tests the RAF had conducted with a Hawker Demon fighter. These trials suggested that a 'broadside' with moveable machine guns was a better way to attack bomber formations than the conventional fixed-gun fighter. The turret fighter would take this idea to extremes by removing any fixed, forward facing armament in order to encourage the pilot to manoeuvre the aircraft to use the turret armament's potential.

The theory that modern fighters were too fast to dogfight, and that the conventional fighter with front facing guns could only manage a single pass against a bomber formation in any encounter, was popular in the late 1930s. This pessimistic view of the ability of fighters to knock down bombers led serendipitously to a massive increase in forward facing armament (the eight-Browning .303in standard for RAF day fighters) but also led experts and policy-makers to devise the concept of a fighter which could fly alongside the bomber formation at the same height and speed while subjecting the bombers to a

The third production Roc, L3059, undergoing testing as a floatplane in December 1939 at the Marine Aeroplane Evaluation Establishment at Helensburgh. The aircraft was tested with a view to using Rocs as catapult-launched air defence (cont..)

* A design study for a Merlin powered turret fighter similar in many respects to the Roc dated 17th April 1935 was prepared, possibly for Specification F.34/35

(Cont...) fighters for warships but the plan was abandoned due to the aircraft's inadequate performance. L3059 has the factory applied Royal Navy 'temperate sea' camouflage scheme initially worn by all front line Rocs. The aircraft was lost on take-off on the 3rd December 1939 as a result of directional instability caused by the floats. L3057 was modified with a deeper strake under the tail, which improved stability. Although the floatplane scheme was never progressed beyond the testing stage, Roc L3174 was later used as a float-based target tug. (BAE Systems)

hail of machine gun fire. The turret fighter was intended to attack unescorted bombers, or act in tandem with conventional interceptors which would keep the fighter escort occupied.

Even the Air Ministry seemed to be getting cold feet about the concept though, as on 25th January 1938 the Admiralty ordered 127 Fairey Fulmars as insurance against the Roc proving a failure. The Roc has often been seen as a naval equivalent of the Boulton Paul Defiant though it was actually used in a manner more closely related to its original intention by complementing conventional fighters. Rocs were issued in small numbers to Skua squadrons, whilst Defiants were forced to act in isolation of the interceptors they were designed to partner. In addition the Roc was intended to act as a float-mounted fighter, catapult launched from battleships to help drive off bombing attacks and shadowing aircraft when there was no aircraft carrier available or to supplement existing fighters.

On 10th July 1937, 136 Rocs were ordered off the drawing board. The Skua had already flown by this time and the Air Ministry and Navy were evidently pleased enough with its performance to procure the turret armed version. In fact, such was the similarity with the Skua that no prototypes were required and the Roc proceeded directly to production.

Blackburn was however mired in the delayed production of the Skua and concurrent production of the Botha. Boulton Paul, whose turret was to be fitted, was therefore contracted on 10th July 1937 to produce the Roc.

Engine installation and fuselage up to the centre section were the same as the Skua, as was the detachable rear section. The wings too were substantially

similar, but had 2° dihedral, no upturn in the tips and lacked the four machine guns. The rear fuselage was widened to accommodate the Boulton Paul Type A Mk II electrically driven turret, and the cockpit aft of the pilot was changed. Gone was the cavernous opening of the Skua and in its place a tiny 'cabin' housing the radio equipment and the observer when he was not manning the turret. The roof of this cabin was automatically lowered whenever the turret was trained forwards to create room for the guns to traverse. Similarly a wedge-shaped fairing aft of the turret lowered into the rear fuselage whenever necessary to allow the guns to traverse.

The attachment of the floats can be viewed in this head on photograph of L3059 during testing. The floats were designed to be easily fitted to all Rocs, which had pick-up points fitted as standard. (BAE Systems)

A very rare image of Roc L3059 carrying out tests as a floatplane, seen here about to 'unstick'. (BAE Systems)

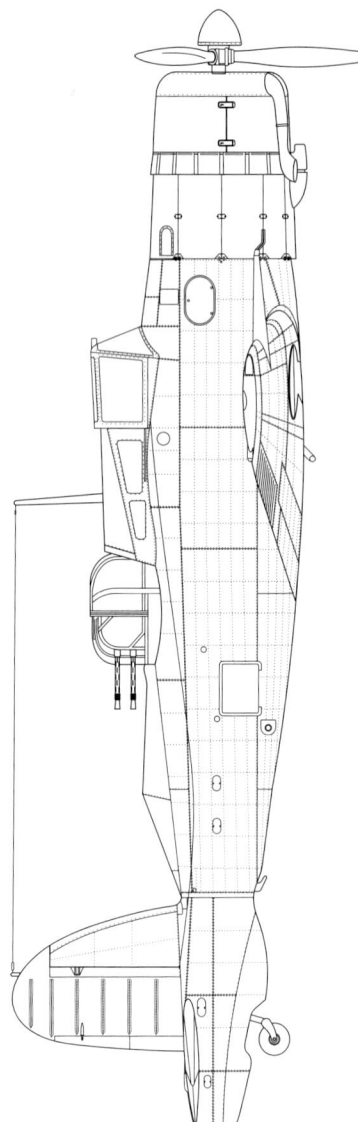

*Blackburn Roc.
1/72 scale.*

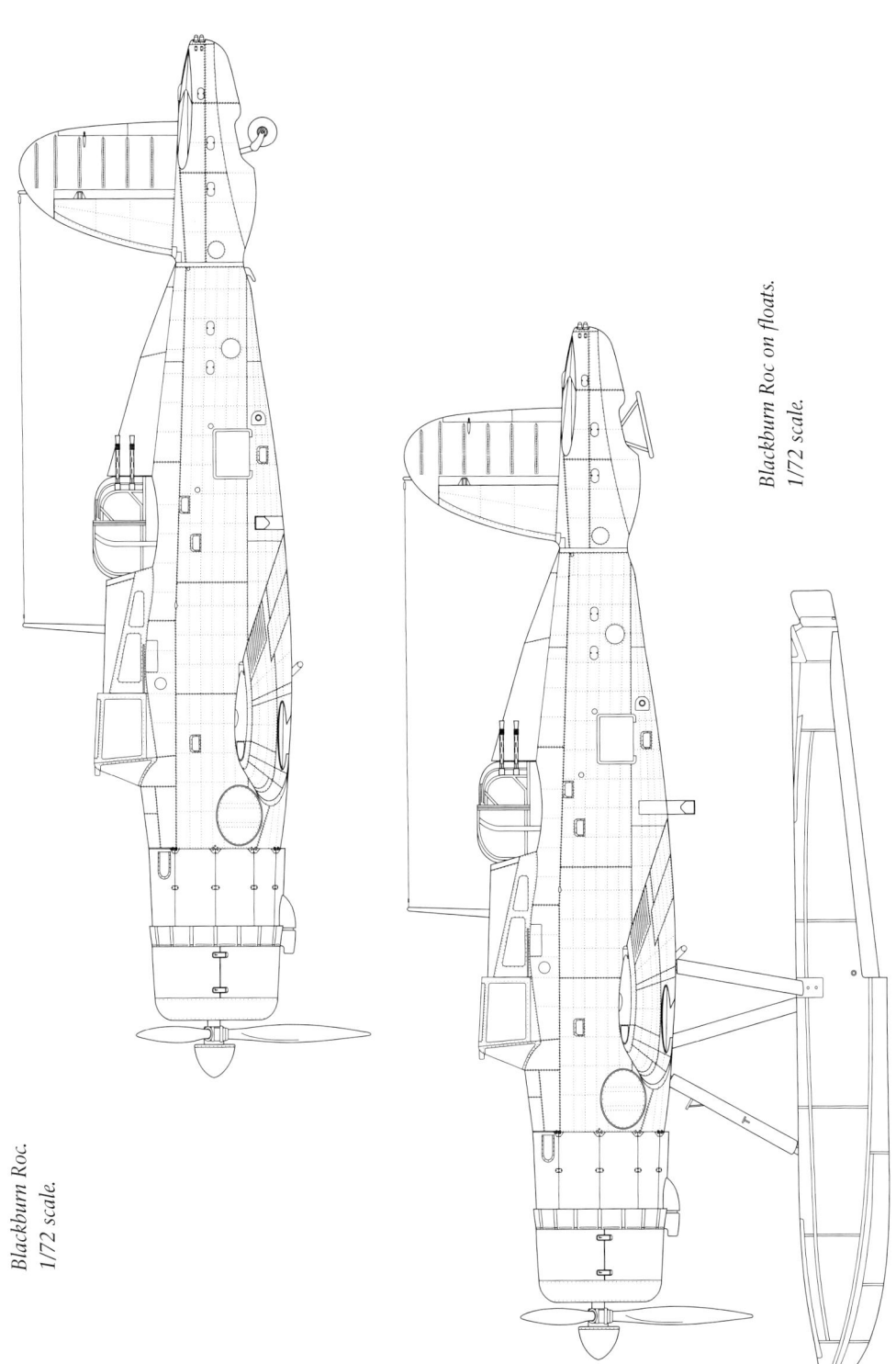

Blackburn Roc. 1/72 scale.

Blackburn Roc on floats. 1/72 scale.

Blackburn Roc.
1/72 scale.

Blackburn Roc on floats. 1/72 scale.

First production Roc (sometimes referred to as Roc prototype) L3057. The turret has not yet received its guns, and the drag reducing fairings are fully extended. The line of the chord to release the anti-spin parachute can be seen running along the starboard fuselage. L3057 was modified into a floatplane and underwent testing in this guise before ending its days as an instructional airframe at No.6 School of Technical Training, Hednesford. (BAE Systems)

As there was less space in the fuselage for fuel, a detachable streamlined 70 gallon tank was designed to be added under the centre section, but it was not ready for service use by the time the Roc was withdrawn from the front line.

Roc L3057 made its first flight on the day before Christmas Eve 1938, at the hands of Blackburn test pilot Flight Lieutenant H.J. Wilson. It remained at Brough for contractor's trials until March 1939 when the A&AEE took it on for handling tests. Stalling speed was rather higher than the Skua but otherwise the handling of the Roc was an improvement. All aerobatic manoeuvres could be performed, but the turret apparently caused the Roc to yaw to the left every time it was moved, regardless of the direction of rotation.

L3057 showed a tendency to blow fuses, and if the turret was used over-exuberantly the air pressure system that operated the drag cheating fairings would run down, meaning the turret could not be fully moved until the pressure had built back up again. L3057 was joined at the A&AEE by L3059, while the second Roc, L3058, was used for turret tests.

Although the Roc's handling was satisfactory, performance left something to be desired. In search of an improvement the A&AEE tried different propellers. L3057 and L3059 took part in comparative tests, one with the Roc's standard de Havilland type 5/8 propeller of 12' diameter and the other using the Skua's 11'6" type 5/10 item. Meanwhile, L3058, which had subsequently joined the two other Rocs, tested a hybrid propeller using a Skua hub and blades from an Armstrong Whitworth Whitley. With this fitted, the rate of climb was improved slightly although there was no increase in speed.

With handling trials largely complete, L3057 and L3059 were converted to floatplane configuration at Dumbarton and sent to the Marine Aeroplane Evaluation Establishment at Helensburgh in November 1939. Specification 20/37 required suitably tank tested parts so that with the appropriate kit any Roc could be converted to a floatplane. The kit consisted of existing Blackburn Shark floats fitted with water rudders and aerodynamically profiled struts and rigging designed to attach to specially designed pick-up points.

The float gear degraded directional stability and L3059 was destroyed in a crash on the 3rd December as a result. Consequently L3057 was fitted with a much deeper fin under the tail. L3060 and L3074 were also converted, but by this time the floatplane's disappointing performance was evident and the idea fell out of favour. Further trials scheduled for June 1940 were cancelled.

The final development work for the Roc was carried out by 759 (training) Squadron in the second half of 1940 to ascertain the best tactical use of the aircraft. Trials included intercommunication and co-operation between pilot and gunner and more general questions of how the Roc would work with other fighters, on which an experienced pilot and air gunner were to be employed. The Air Staff and the Admiralty still felt that the turret fighter offered greater potential than the Skua for short range interception. The following comments by Admiral Forbes, C-in-C of the Home Fleet are illuminating. 'The Roc as a free gun fighter with an excellent multi-gun turret is more than superior to the Skua; it offers the only chance of effective action against an enemy aircraft of equal or superior performance. To be effective, the fixed gun fighter must have a superior performance and, unless vastly superior, is confined in attack to a limited arc of approach, thus making the defensive armouring of the enemy comparatively easy. Fleet Air Arm fighters are unlikely to have such superiority and it is therefore recommended that such fighters should in future be either wholly free gun turret fighters or perhaps fitted with one large calibre fixed gun in addition'[1]. By the end of the year operational experience had shown the Roc to have little use as a fighter and investigations were discontinued. It is with hindsight surprising how much faith was placed in the flawed concept of the turret fighter, but the experience of the crews, as outlined later, show how divorced concept and reality were.

---

1   *Documents from the National Archives under ADM1/1074 9, 11th February 1940.*

The 'Pit Ponies'

Late in 1938, the Fleet Air Arm's most senior unit, 800 Naval Air Squadron, received three of the new Blackburn Skua Mk II fighter dive-bombers. The aircraft were received in time for HMS *Ark Royal*'s spring cruise and 800 Squadron spent the next few months evaluating the new aircraft alongside the existing Hawker Ospreys and Nimrods.

By August of 1939, 800 Squadron's strength had increased to six Skuas, and 803 Squadron had also received its first six Skuas. Initially, both squadrons were based at Royal Naval Air Station Worthy Down, a former bomber station which had a target marked on the grass and quadrant positions on the perimeter. The squadrons training on the new aircraft in the relatively unfamiliar art of dive bombing made good use of the target.

Captain Eric Brown describes the technique developed during this period. The Skuas would '…approach the target at about 8,000ft at right angles, keeping it in sight until it disappeared under the leading edge of the wingtip, pulling up until it reappeared at the trailing edge and then winging over into a 70 degree dive, extending the Zap flaps fully and keeping the target at the top of the engine cowling. Release height was 3,000ft and pull-out was commenced, simultaneously retracting the flaps, being completed at around 1,500ft to avoid the bomb blast and any light flak.'[1]

Usually, the attack would be made from up-sun, or if this was not practicable, four flights would approach from separate directions 90 degrees apart, each flight aiming to hit the target just after the last had done so.

Skua L2887 'A7F' of 803 Squadron demonstrating colourful pre-war markings of Ark Royal's air group in 1939. Note the practice bomb carried in a Light Series bomb rack beneath the port wing. (Fleet Air Arm Museum)

Skua L2933 in colourful pre-war markings. This aircraft was operated by 800 Squadron from Ark Royal in 1939 and flown by Lieutenant K.V. Spurway. Light series bomb carriers are fitted beneath the wings. The coloured tail may denote a flight-leader's aircraft. (K.V. Spurway, via Fleet Air Arm Museum)

As a modern monoplane with dive brakes and other unfamiliar devices the Skua was something of a leap for the pilots, although most got used to the new aircraft remarkably easily. Lieutenant B.S. McEwan of 803 Squadron is reported to have exclaimed "My God, this is an old tank!" when he collected his L2873 from Blackburn's at Brough[2]. After they had become accustomed to the flaps and multi-pitch propeller, the pilots generally found the Skua to be easy to fly and pleasant to handle, and swiftly discovered its abilities as a dive bomber. 'From 3,000ft I half-rolled, with full flaps, and dived vertically – vertically, not just steeply… Then I eased her out of the dive, flattening out easily at 50ft, and lifting those wonderful flaps for a zoom to gain altitude; no sign of squash or high speed stalling,' enthused Pilot Officer D.H. Clarke, an RAF pilot who flew Skuas with No. 2 AA Co-operation Unit based at Gosport.

Training on the Skua on its introduction was not the well-planned and integrated process that would be developed during the war. Existing pilots had the most cursory of introductions to the aircraft. Captain (later Major) R.T. Partridge RM was introduced to the Skua on 18th October 1939 with a ten minute flight in the back seat of L2914 with 758 Squadron. Later that afternoon, he went solo. Even when training had been more formalised, it depended on the squadron as to what was covered. Many training squadrons did not teach dive bombing techniques, though some did, and dive bombing training was often left to be covered by the operational squadrons – a task which became virtually impossible once war had commenced in earnest.

Individual pilots were also left to develop the technique that suited them best in dive bombing. "Some pilots lowered their strong flaps for the dive. I did not, preferring to descend as fast as I could, knowing that the Skua was a wonderfully steady aircraft," said Lieutenant C.H. Filmer, who took part in two of the Skua's most famous dive bombing attacks with 803 Squadron.[3]

A flight of 803 Squadron Skuas in the colourful pre-war schemes worn by many Ark Royal aircraft, possibly off the south coast of England. All Skuas were delivered from the factory in all-over silver dope and it was up to squadrons to apply their own markings - tail bands on A7F (L2887) probably denote a flight-leader's aircraft. (Stratus collection)

By the end of August, a third squadron, 801 NAS, was working up on the Skua and due to join HMS *Furious* in October, while *Ark Royal*'s squadrons had moved to RNAS Hatston on Orkney. Nevertheless, the squadron was soon ready for operations. It was not a moment too soon, as the movements of German warships into the North Sea and the Atlantic made it all but certain that the Fleet Air Arm was soon to be at war. On 28th August, 800 and 803 squadrons under Lieutenant G.N. Torry and Lieutenant Commander D.R.F. Cambell respectively began patrolling north of the Shetlands to check for movement of German naval and merchant units. Five days later, Britain was at war. *Ark Royal*'s crews were rapidly recalled before the ship sailed for war, resulting in something of a 'pier-head jump' for many. Petty Officer R.S. 'Dickie' Rolph committed the cardinal naval sin of volunteering when he put his name forward for a Skua squadron – and was rewarded with the post of Senior TAG on 800 Squadron. Less happily, he was recalled from honeymoon to take up the post! 'The flight deck was a picture – the armourers' nightmare. Bombs in wooden crates, bombs loose, 303 belted ammo, planes, torpedoes strewn over the flight deck – all of which finally went to its appointed place below,' said Rolph.[4]

Ark Royal with its two Skua squadrons, along with the Home Fleet's other aircraft carriers, *Furious* and *Courageous*, were initially employed on anti submarine duties in the North Sea. It was dangerous work for such valuable ships, as they were soon to find out. On 14th September, *Ark Royal* received word that the steamer *Fanad Head* was being attacked by a U-boat, and launched three Skuas equipped with 100lb anti-submarine bombs.

The Skuas patrolled individually, and the first found the *Fanad Head* while U-30 was attempting to sink it with guns. They attacked the rapidly diving U-boat, only to damage themselves with their own bomb blast and have to ditch. The second aircraft stumbled on the scene and, amazingly, was also damaged by its own bomb and forced to ditch. The third Skua then found the ship and the submarine and strafed the latter before returning to *Ark Royal*. Both pilots of the ditched Skuas survived and were taken on board the U-boat, gaining the dubious honour of being the first naval airmen to become Prisoners of War. One rear gunner was killed in the crash while another was wounded and died in the water. It has been suggested that the pilots flew too low when releasing their bombs, although it is also possible that the bombs were fused with insufficient delay.*

Almost as soon as the aircraft had flown off, *Ark Royal* herself was narrowly missed by two torpedoes from another U-boat. If this wasn't enough to prove the folly of the anti-submarine work, *Courageous* was sunk three days later and the patrols were brought to an end.

It was an inauspicious start to the Skua's career in action, but things improved before the month was out. On 26th September *Ark Royal* was patrolling in the North Sea, 250 miles north-west of Heligoland. A reconnaissance flight reported that aircraft were shadowing the fleet and a flight of 800 Squadron Skuas, led by Lieutenant Kindersley, was despatched to deal with them. The effective radar-directed fighter control systems had not been developed this early in the war and in the poor visibility the Ark had to direct the Skuas onto the shadower, a Dornier Do18 flying boat, by visual signals, morse wireless-telegraphy and pyrotechnics. A second sub-flight was launched led by Lieutenant Finch-Noyes when a second Dornier was reported, and both flights eventually found their targets and made a series of attacks. The Dorniers were driven off but their diesel engines could take a great deal of punishment and keep running, and they escaped. However, a third Dornier was forced down by another flight of 803 Squadron Skuas led by Lieutenant Charles Evans, a 'dashing, fiery sailor, and one of the Navy's finest fighter pilots'.[5] The Skuas attacked from

The aircrew of 800 Naval Air Squadron posed before a Skua, possibly while the squadron was working up in the Mediterranean in late 1938 or while sailing to the South Atlantic shortly after the outbreak of war. (Courtesy of Denis Rolph)

---

* A detailed account of this mission can be found on John Dell's Skua website http://freespace.virgin.net/john.dell/blackburn_skua.htm

A Skua demonstrates the tight fit with Ark Royal's lifts. As the engine is still running it seems this aircraft has just landed – before Ark Royal adopted the crash barrier each Skua had to be rapidly struck down and removed from the flight deck before the next could land. This is in the South Atlantic during the chase for Graf Spee. (Fleet Air Arm Museum)

astern, opening up with the four Browning machine guns, before breaking away so the observer could rake the target with the rear gun. The Dornier ditched and the crew were taken off by HMS *Somali*, which then sank the flying boat with its guns. This was the first enemy aircraft confirmed destroyed by British forces in the war and was credited to 'Horse' Seymour, McEwen's TAG and a pre-war gunnery expert.*

What happened next marked a watershed in Fleet Air Arm fighter tactics. The shadowers had reported the fleet's position during the chase with the Skuas and within hours a gaggle of twin-engined bombers appeared overhead. However, rather than being given the chance to add to their now-opened score, the Skuas were struck down in the hangers and drained of fuel to lessen the risk of fire. This act reflected the Navy's pre-war theorising that fleet defence was the job of the anti-aircraft gun and partly explains the casual treatment of the role of the fighter in Specification 0.27/34.

Of the five aircraft that attacked the *Ark Royal*, one got close enough to drop a 2,000lb bomb 30 yards from the carrier's bow. Dickie Rolph described the incident: 'We had our scares such as when a twin engined aircraft (reported on the bridge as "OK Air, it's an Anson") made a bombing attack by dropping a 2,000lb bomb – the captain of *Ark Royal* was very quick off the mark and increased speed and ordered "hard-a-starboard". The bomb went over the port bow as the ship swung to starboard and exploded some little distance off. The He111** pulled up and dropped her other bombs and in a final defiant

* *This was not quite the first aircraft shot down, as a bomber had been destroyed some days earlier by RAF Battles, but this was not confirmed until after the 26th*

** *Although contemporary identification said that the attacking bombers were Heinkel He111s, it was in fact more likely that they were Junkers Ju88s of I KG30. I am indebted to John Dell for pointing out that Ju88s were heavily used for anti-shipping raids at this time and*

gesture came down and machine-gunned the flight deck, giving '*Ark*' its only war-wound – a bullet dent in the after round-down'. The C-in-C is alleged to have signalled the fleet 'For God's sake buck up and shoot the thing down!'[6] The *Ark* was unharmed though the near miss was enough for Dr. Goebbels to claim that the carrier had been blown up - and for the Admiralty to insist that fighters be launched to defend the fleet, even if only to contribute to the disruption of any attack.

At the beginning of October, 801 Squadron began a three month cruise with *Furious*. 803 Squadron disembarked *Ark Royal* at Scapa Flow and 800 Squadron remained on board while the carrier was despatched to the South Atlantic in the hunt for the pocket battleship *Graf Spee*, which was causing severe damage to commerce.

This cruise could have given the Skuas the chance to test their dive-bombing mettle against a large, armoured ship, but a chance course change by the *Graf Spee* on 24th October put the *Ark Royal*'s patrols slightly out of range and the raider went undetected. As it was, the Skua crews spent most of the time cooling their heels while the Swordfish squadrons patrolled millions of miles of sea. Captain A.J. Power was unwilling to let the Skuas go out of sight of the ship on the few occasions they were allowed to launch. Apart from some exercises were concentrated on the North Sea coast. Very little was known by British forces about the Ju88 in the early stages of the war and it was not surprising that the twin-engined aircraft were misidentified as Heinkels.

The long range ventral fuel tank which was undergoing development for the Roc but ultimately did not become available before the aircraft was withdrawn from frontline use. The streamlined 70-gallon belly tank was designed to be detachable but could not be jettisoned in flight. (BAE Systems)

in which the Skuas made mock attacks on Swordfish returning from patrol, all the Skua crews gained from this period was the unflattering nickname 'the Pit Ponies' in recognition of all the time they spent in the hangar.

Some of 800 Squadron's old guard did not let this get to them however. Lieutenant Finch-Noyes formed '*Ark Royal* Productions' which staged theatrical entertainments and, later, 'radio' broadcasts on the ship's tannoy. A Christmas revue was staged in which the lieutenant appeared as the Faery Queen, suspended in a parachute! The squadron sat out the Battle of the River Plate while *Ark Royal* and the rest of Force H steamed hard to intercept. Another half-chance for the squadron's Skuas to attack a major warship at sea evaporated when, instead of fighting the British forces stationed off the Uruguayan coast, the *Graf Spee*'s crew scuttled her on December 17th. At the end of January *Ark Royal* saluted the cruiser squadron which had defeated the powerful German warship on their return to Britain. A flight of Skuas performed a formation dive and low level flypast, close enough for the crews to see HMS *Exeter*'s splinter-riddled upperworks and turret patched with corrugated iron. It was as close as 800 Squadron would get to combat in the South Atlantic.

In October, 801 Squadron embarked on *Furious* for a three month cruise and provided fighter cover for the first Canadian convoy. Back in Britain, 803 Squadron flew to Wick in Scotland after they had disembarked. The Squadron's eight Skuas and four Rocs were solely responsible for protecting the Home Fleet anchorage at Scapa Flow from bombing attacks until the middle of December. Direct attacks on Scapa did not materialise quite as expected and 803 were often required to intercept enemy aircraft further out to sea. The Skuas and Rocs were needed to deal with aircraft shadowing or attacking the Home Fleet at sea, trawlers and convoys, sometimes over 200 miles away.

The lower performance and endurance of the Rocs was a problem - in many cases these aircraft had to turn back before contact with the enemy had been

One of 37 Rocs earmarked for sending to Finland in 1940. This one has been given the Finnish code RO-150, and painted with Finnish national markings (which may have been overpainted with temporary distemper for transit) over the British roundels. In all other respects the Roc appears to be in early wartime factory finish temperate sea scheme. (Fleet Air Arm Museum)

made. In January 1940, Lieutenant Commander Cambell commanding 803 requested that the Rocs be replaced with more Skuas, but Commander in Chief of the Home Fleet and the Admiralty resisted, on the basis that 803 was the only squadron operating Rocs and able to explore the possible tactical uses of the turret fighter. With some RAF squadrons and 804 Naval Air Squadron now available for defence of the northern naval bases, 803 was increasingly required to perform long range fighter patrols to protect shipping. The long range fuel tank for the Rocs was still under development and 803 Squadron often found itself short on strength after the Rocs had to turn for home leaving the Skuas to carry on. The turret fighters were found to have an endurance of between two hours 45 minutes and three hours only, compared with anything up to four and a half hours for the Skua.

However, in early 1940 the Air Ministry proposed giving 33 Rocs to the Finnish Air Force, who were fighting the 'Winter War' against the Soviet Union. The fighters were assembled at Dyce in Scotland with Finnish serials painted over the Fleet Air Arm numbers and roundels hastily painted out with white discs and Finnish symbols in pale blue. The Finns were arch improvisers and made good use of such unlikely machinery as the Morane-Saulnier MS406 and Brewster Buffalo, so it is tempting to consider what might have been achieved. As the Rocs were due to be sent out, the Winter War ended and the delivery was cancelled.

In February 1940 Lieutenant Commander Charles Evans, late of 803 Squadron, formed the fourth frontline Skua and Roc unit, 806 Squadron at Worthy Down. In March, 806 moved to Hatston on Orkney, joining 803 which had moved there from Wick, and 800 which disembarked from *Ark Royal* following the return from the South Atlantic. When 801's North Atlantic cruise concluded they disembarked at Evanton.

Four of the Rocs assembled at Dyce in Scotland where they were to be sent to Finland to fight against the Soviet Union. This plan was cancelled when the 'Winter War' ended. Three of the Rocs are in naval camouflage, but the fourth appears to have a darker colour scheme. All wear what appear to be pale discs covering the British roundels, though unlike other photographs, no Finnish national markings are apparent. (Fleet Air Arm Museum)

Early in 1940 in the North Sea convoys and naval units came under increasing pressure from enemy bombers looking for targets of opportunity or directed to targets by reconnaissance aircraft or U-boats. It was while defending shipping against these threats that 803 Squadron, now led by Lieutenant William Paulet Lucy, started to develop the offensive techniques that later reached their peak in Norway.

A combat report by Lucy from March 1940 demonstrates a typical mission performed by 803 during this period: 'Weather was clear with about 10/10 cloud at 3000 ft. In places the cloud was down to 500ft but not near the scene of the combat. Enemy aircraft was flying low, alone around some small merchant ships. It appeared to be firing at the waterline. Tracer bullets could be clearly seen.

'Our first attack was fairly steep diving attack. E/A [Enemy Aircraft] was making off, climbing and turning slowly to port. E/A opened fire first, all shots passing to port. Our fighter opened with short bursts, the first appeared slightly astern and the second ahead of the E/A. A later burst appeared to enter the E/A's fuselage and the rear gun ceased firing. The enemy was overhauled and our fighter turned to starboard. E/A was attacked again [and] considerable deflection [was] used as E/A was still turning to port. As the range came to about 50 yards the E/A was enveloped in a cloud of black smoke and it was thought that it had burst into flames. This was not the case however, as our observer saw E/A climb into cloud with his undercarriage down... Very considerable slipstream effect was found at the close range of 50 yards, it threw our aircraft off its aim at the end of both attacks.'[7]

The 'steep diving attack' and extremely close range achieved when firing on the bomber were characteristic of the practices employed by Skua pilots to compensate for their aircraft's slow level speed and relatively light armament. The Skua's high diving speed and stability meant that if pilots were able to

An unidentified Roc believed to be at Eastleigh between January and March 1940. The all-black colour scheme is intriguing but the reason for it unknown. Eastleigh was home to the 759 Squadron, part of the No.1 Naval Fighter Training School in early 1940 – this unit was charged with trialling the best tactical use of the Roc. Note the ground-crew holding the tail down. (Captain PCS Chilton AFC, RN, courtesy of Pat Chilton and Steven Jefferson)

A distinctly worn-looking Skua taking off at Eastleigh in early 1940, sans rear gunner. The reason for the black colour scheme is unknown but a number of naval aircraft based at Eastleigh appear to have had similar schemes applied. The degradation of the paint behind the cockpit is reminiscent of the 'Special Night' paint developed for night fighters around this time which was vulnerable to wear and damage. (Captain PCS Chilton AFC, RN, courtesy of Pat Chilton and Steven Jefferson)

get into the right position before an attack they could easily overhaul aircraft that under other circumstances could use superior speed to escape. However, the hell-for-leather dive and extreme close range attacks were not without their risks and Skua pilots had precious little protection against return fire. Armoured seat protection and windscreen glass was not at that time standard equipment on British fighters, though the RAF was already stockpiling armour for Hurricanes and Spitfires.

The U-boat threat was still very much apparent and on 12th March 1940, Blue Flight of 803 Squadron, again led by Lucy, attacked a submarine off the coast of Scotland. The first two aircraft dropped 100lb bombs and the first was seen to explode close to where the U-boat had submerged. The second also fell on target but was not observed to have exploded. Although later experience showed that bombs exploding below the surface could not always be seen to detonate, it is also true that the reliability of British bombs at the beginning of the war left something to be desired, with the 100lb AS bomb being particularly poor.

Ark Royal's other Skua unit, 800 Squadron, was also engaged in convoy protection while the carrier was training its Swordfish squadrons in the Mediter-

Two Rocs at Eastleigh in early 1940. Eastleigh was home to several Fleet Air Arm fighter training and development squadrons which could be the reason for the presence of these aircraft. The left hand Roc retains the all-over silver scheme that the development aircraft were finished in, suggesting it is one of the earliest Rocs produced. The right hand Roc appears to be painted in a single all-over colour, though it is not clear what this might be. (Captain PCS Chilton AFC, RN, courtesy of Pat Chilton and Steven Jefferson)

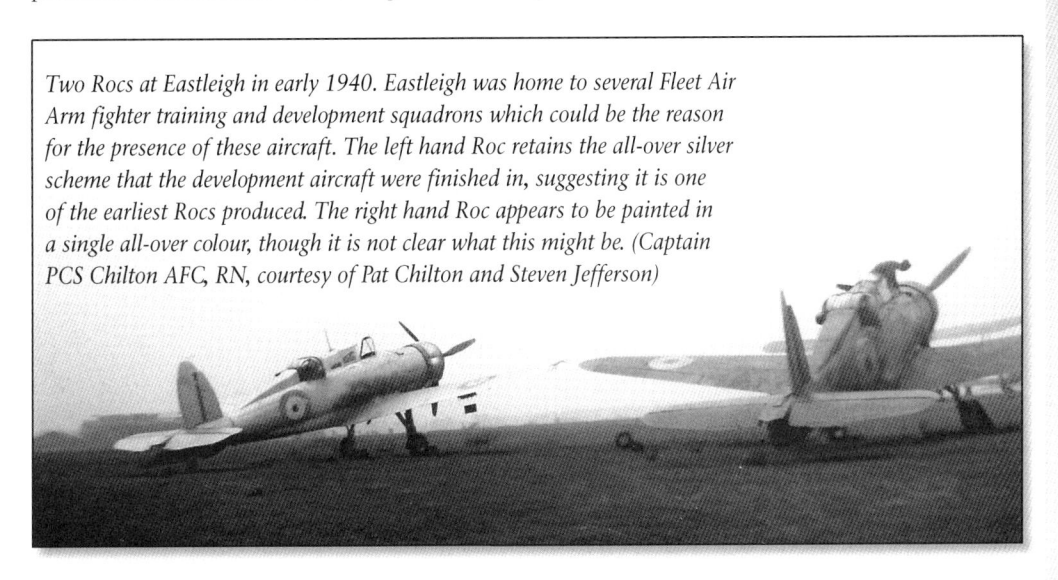

A Skua 'running-up' at Eastleigh in early 1940. This aircraft appears to have had its factory silver finish over painted with black, which has worn and chipped considerably around the wing leading edge and the gun ports. It wears Type-A roundels beneath the wings. In company are a number of Gladiators and a Percival Gull on the far left. (Captain PCS Chilton AFC, RN, courtesy of Pat Chilton and Steven Jefferson)

ranean. Attacks were becoming bolder, to the extent that on 20th March Green Flight intercepted ten Heinkel He111s (possibly Junkers Ju88s – see footnote on previous page) bombing convoy ON21 just 20 miles from Orkney. On this occasion, as on many others, the Skuas were not able to shoot down any of the bombers, but possibly damaged some and disrupted the attack.

Lieutenant Commander Torry handed over command of the squadron to the Royal Marine Captain R.T. Partridge on 1st April 1940, at the end of five days of attacks on the fleet anchorage at Scapa Flow. During this period the Skua squadrons had driven off many bomber attacks but there were few confirmed claims - one bomber shot down and several damaged, including the first claim by a Roc.* The 'phoney war' was well and truly behind the Skuas and Rocs, but they were about to enter the most eventful period of their career over Norway.

1   Captain Eric Brown, *Wings of the Navy*, p.30
2   Kenneth Poolman, *Ark Royal*, p.38
3   Letter from C.H. Filmer to the author 10th December 2006
4   R.S. Rolph BEM, *unpublished memoir That First Phoney Year* reproduced by kind permission of Denis Rolph
5   Kenneth Poolman, *Ark Royal*, p.58
6   R.S. Rolph BEM, *unpublished memoir That First Phoney Year*
7   803 Squadron Diaries from the National Archives under AIR 50/321

---

*   It has frequently been quoted that the Roc never went into action and never flew from an aircraft carrier, the fault lying with that most august of sources, Putnam's 'Blackburn Aircraft Since 1909'. Neither statement is correct.

Another mysteriously dark Skua thought to be from Eastleigh between January and March 1940. It carries light series bomb racks beneath the wings. In the background a number of other aircraft can be seen, including a Hawker Audax and Blackburn Rocs. (Captain PCS Chilton AFC, RN, courtesy of Pat Chilton and Steven Jefferson)

Another of the all-black Skuas and Rocs at Eastleigh. What may be a Type-B roundel can be seen on the heavily worn rear fuselage, and Type-A roundels on the wing undersides. The aircraft does not appear to carry any codes or serial. It possibly belongs to one of the fighter naval training and development schools based at Eastleigh on the South coast of England at this time. (Captain PCS Chilton AFC, RN, courtesy of Pat Chilton and Steven Jefferson)

Norway

On 8th April 1940, the German high command set Operation *Weserübung* – The invasion of neutral Norway and Denmark – in motion. These countries had been on friendly terms with Germany, and the savagery of the attack caught defences in those countries almost literally napping. Six groups of warships under Vice-Admiral Lütjens struck out during the night to occupy key Norwegian ports and cities so swiftly as to overwhelm any resistance and establish defences against a counter attack by the British and French navies. In fact, Norway had been fiercely resistant to Allied presence before the attack. Plans to support Finland by transporting troops and equipment through Sweden had been strongly objected to by the Norwegian government, and the British and French had even mooted an allied occupation of Norway. The following day German forces had taken Denmark without a shot having been fired. Most of Norway was under German control, and only at Oslo had they suffered serious losses when the heavy cruiser *Blücher* was sunk by the capital's ancient Krupp artillery.

What followed was the first battle in history where land, sea and air forces all played a major part, and all four operational Skua squadrons would prove to be central to the Allied counter attack. However, at the outset the RN was caught so entirely off guard that the only carrier available was *Furious*, and it had no fighters as 801 Squadron was ashore at Evanton. The other two operational Skua squadrons were at Hatston while their carriers were in the Mediterranean, training - 806 Squadron was still working up.

The cruiser Königsberg was a fast, well armed ship of around 7,500 tons, and was used during the invasion of Norway to take Bergen. The ship was tied up against the Skoltegrund Mole in the harbour on the 10th April when Skuas of 800 and 803 Squadrons dive bombed her, scoring numerous hits. She sank in less than two hours. (John Asmussen via Kjetil Aakra)

As soon as the invasion had taken place, various plans were mooted to counter attack, focussing on Bergen where two 6in gun cruisers of the *Köln* class had forced the harbour. A naval raid was planned and cancelled, while an attack by Swordfish from *Furious* was overruled as too dangerous without fighters to protect the carrier. The Home Fleet, moving close to the Norwegian coast, was soon under heavy attack from waves of Junkers Ju87 Stukas, which sank the destroyer *Ghurka* and damaged other ships. The task force was obviously vulnerable without fighter cover, even with the considerable anti-aircraft batteries available to them.

The RAF bombed Bergen harbour in the evening of 9th April, but caused no damage to the ships there. However, RAF photo reconnaissance of the harbour earlier that day planted the seed of another mission. Lieutenant Commander Geoffrey Hare, 800 Squadron Senior Observer, was attached to RAF Coastal Command at the time (as many RN observers were for ship-recognition purposes) and was in the reconnaissance Blenheim that overflew Bergen and reported the two *Köln*s. He suggested Skuas would have a good chance of inflicting serious damage on the ships. Commander C.L. Howe, officer in charge of RNAS Hatston, approved the scheme and the Director of Naval Air Division (DNAD) rubber-stamped the proposals. The Skuas were all set for an attack on the morning of the 10th, little more than a day after the invasion.

Hare himself flew on the mission as Captain Partridge's observer. The two squadron commanders, with Hare and Commander Howe, decided that the Skuas should take off at night and attack at sunrise to give them the best chance

A Roc pilot signs a flying chit before taking to the air in L3147. A small number of Rocs saw service during the Norwegian campaigns, which was the only time the turret fighters operated from aircraft carriers. (BAE Systems)

What the Skua does best; a single aircraft demonstrates the Skua's ability to maintain a steady, steep dive to place its bomb with unerring accuracy as sixteen Skuas of 800 and 803 Squadrons achieved on the 10th April 1940 when they sank the cruiser Königsberg.

of surprise. This required faultless night-time formation flying and navigation, as Bergen lay some two hours away from Hatston at the Skua's cruising speed, leaving precious little spare endurance. During the night, the cruiser *Köln* had left Bergen, leaving her sister the *Königsberg* tied up against the mole, remaining because of faulty machinery. This cruiser was fast and powerful for her size with a battery of nine six inch guns and a maximum speed of 32kt, and had been one of the first ships built under Germany's post First World War rearmament programme.

Aircrew briefing took place following a certain amount of secrecy; 'until we saw our armourers loading up 500lb bombs when we knew something was definitely on,' said 'Dickie' Rolph[1]. At 0500 eleven Skuas of 803 Squadron and five of 800 Squadron took off with a full load of fuel and ammunition and a 500lb SAP bomb apiece. 'The Skua, when fully loaded, needed all the runway that Hatston could provide and once airborne behaved like a pregnant porpoise,' Rolph added. They formed up at 3,000ft in two flights of seven and nine. They climbed slowly to 10,000ft and proceeded east at 140kt, the Skua's most economical speed. Cloud cover steadily increased, and Captain Partridge's column lost touch with Lieutenant Lucy's so both navigated independently to the target.

Shortly after 0640 the Norwegian coast was sighted, and the Skuas swung north to approach Bergen. At about 0700 they sighted the slim profile of the cruiser lying against the pier. 803 Squadron arrived first and skirted the harbour to attack out of the sun from 8,000ft. Anti-aircraft defences were caught completely by surprise and half the aircraft completed their attack before any of the guns even started firing. This was fortunate as the *Königsberg* was particularly well equipped with AA defences. In fact the forces at Bergen had been told that the only single-engined aircraft in the area were friendly.

Fortuitously, 800 Squadron arrived on their bomb run just as 803 Squadron were finishing theirs, apart from one aircraft which had become separated and attacked independently. Because of the lack of resistance, most aircraft were able to perform textbook dives, between 60 and 70 degrees, releasing their bombs between 3,000ft and 1,500ft. Lieutenant Church even went round for a second dive as he was unhappy with his approach the first time, though he encountered rather fiercer anti-aircraft fire the second time and received a holed wing for his trouble.

Lieutenant C.H. Filmer of 803 Squadron noted '… by keeping the whole length of the vessel in front of me was of great assistance in determining when to release the bomb. I tried to keep as close to 60 degrees in my dive simply because it suited my approach… The lower and closer I got the more confident I became. I was very low when I pressed the button'.[2]

The Skua's bombing had been remarkably accurate. Three direct hits were scored – one bomb hit the deck abaft the middle turret, another struck the forecastle and a third struck the most spectacular blow with a bomb right between the *Königsberg*'s funnels. In addition, most of the other bombs were near misses. Several which hit the mole may have skipped onto the ship causing further damage, as (remarkably) the Kriegsmarine actually admitted to more direct hits than the RN claimed. At least one further bomb landed very close to the hull and exploded below the waterline, and the hydrostatic effect helped to seal the cruiser's fate. The DNAD's report noted that the average error had been 50 yards – better even than pre-war training statistics indicated was possible.

The *Königsberg* was well ablaze by the time the Skuas were on their way home and the fire crews were unable to get the flames under control. The ship started to sink by the head, then fifty minutes later rolled over and submerged by the mole.

Roc L3186 in 1940. This picture demonstrates a variation on the Fleet Air Arm's early war 'temperate sea' camouflage pattern, similar to that applied to most Skuas and Rocs from June 1940 - though the aircraft retains night/white wing undersides and no underwing roundels. The clean appearance and lack of exhaust staining suggests the aircraft is either new or recently repainted The turret contains nether guns or equipment, and is facing forwards. (BAE Systems)

A Skua of 800 Squadron begins its take-off run from Ark Royal. Skuas from this squadron operated from the carrier between November 1939 and April 1941. Note the bomb lying on the deck in the foreground – possibly a 500lb SAP device like that used to attack the Königsberg and Scharnhorst. (Fleet Air Arm Museum)

After a tense wait at the rendezvous for the late returning Church, the Skuas set off home. All the aircraft had got out safely even though several had received hits from light flak. However on the return flight Lieutenant B.J. Smeeton's Skua suddenly entered a vertical dive and hit the sea. Both he and Observer Midshipman Watkinson were killed. The most likely explanations for the crash are flak damage to the aircraft's controls or that Smeeton himself had been wounded and later fell unconscious at the controls.

This loss was a blow but despite that the crews had been remarkably lucky. Their luck held yet again over the empty expanses of the North Sea when Hare, navigating for the squadrons, thought they might be lost. 'My worst moment came when returning via Sumburgh (in case anyone wanted to land) and visibility had closed in to about a hazy five miles,' Hare later wrote to Partridge[3]. 'Sumburgh failed to materialise on time on my D.R. [dead reckoning]. I got the horrible sensation that I might be leading the squadrons through the Fair Isle Channel without sighting land'. Faced with the prospect of ploughing on into the grey wastes above Scotland, Hare started to consider a course change – then 'a moment or two later, Sumburgh hove in sight. My relief was intense – no aids to navigation in those days'. The Skuas landed at Hatston at 0945, having stretched their endurance to the accepted limits and beyond.

Despite the BBC erroneously attributing the success to the RAF, the true significance of the attack was obvious to many. The Vice-Admiral of the Orkney and Shetland forces Sir Hugh Binney said: 'this was, I think, the first occasion on which Skuas had been used in action for the real purpose for which they were designed, viz., a dive-bombing attack on an enemy warship. The ship was sunk, the attack was a complete success and I consider that it was brilliantly executed.'[4]

Though this operation has often been considered the Skua's crowning glory, it was really just the opening salvo of the Norwegian campaign that would see almost daily operations in support of sea and land forces until the end of 1940, well after the counter-invasion had ended.

HMS *Glorious* left the Mediterranean for Norway at this point, and *Ark Royal* followed shortly afterwards. The Skuas from Hatston had proved their worth and two days after their attack on Bergen 800 and 803 Squadrons made a second dive bombing attack on the port to add to the damage they had done and further harass the forces there. Again, a single aircraft was lost but the crew, Petty Officer Gardner and Naval Airman Todd, survived and were harboured by locals who took them to the Allied lines. On 14th April, joined by 801 Squadron, the Skuas returned to dive bomb shipping in the harbour, while further north, HMS *Furious* moved to Narvik as without fighters it was safer for her there than in the latitudes of Åndalsnes and Trondheim.

German dive bombing was proving as destructive in Norway as it had in Poland. On 17th April the British cruiser HMS *Suffolk* was subjected to an onslaught which saw her limping away from the field of action with her quarterdeck awash. Skuas from Hatston were despatched to cover *Suffolk*'s return and to protect her in case the Luftwaffe came back to finish the job. The Luftwaffe did indeed return, in force, and aircraft of 803 Squadron shared the destruction of a Heinkel He111 while driving off the rest of the attack. The other two Skua squadrons at Hatston contributed to the protection and destroyed a Dornier Do17, damaged a Do18 and a further three He111s.

The practice of whole-squadron attacks on Norwegian targets was changed slightly around this time in favour of 'offensive reconnaissance' missions, whereby single armed Skuas were sent to reconnoitre for possible targets and attack targets of opportunity, basically a sop to the Admiralty to demonstrate that permanent attack was being maintained. These continued until the 20th when *Ark Royal* and *Glorious* were finally able to embark their fighter squadrons

Lieutenant Callingham's Skua L3048, which ran low on fuel after dive bombing Trondheim harbour. Callingham force landed on Spillrumstranda beach, near Namsos and the Skua was blown up on May 1st by British forces to prevent it falling into enemy hands. (Øyvind Leonsen collection)

and leave for Norway as part of the Norway Campaign Task Force, with Vice-Admiral Wells commanding the aircraft carriers in the squadron. Each of *Ark Royal*'s fighter squadrons 800 and 801 were equipped with nine Skuas, while in addition 801 Squadron brought three Rocs and 800 Squadron had two of the turret fighters. On *Glorious*, 803 Squadron had 11 Skuas, supplemented by the 18 Sea Gladiators of 802 and 804 Squadrons.

The Skua and Roc crews had not operated from an aircraft carrier since January, in the case of 801 and 800 Squadrons, and the previous year in the case of 803, while 806 Squadron had not yet operated from an aircraft carrier and were waiting for HMS *Illustrious* to commission. In fact, many of the pilots had never deck landed a Skua (including Captain Partridge, 800's Officer Commanding), and some had never deck landed at all! It did not help that conditions were dull and squally when the first wave landed on *Ark Royal* on the 22nd. Rear Admiral William Jameson noted 'some of the pilots were evidently inexperienced in deck work, for their arrival was often awesome to behold'![5] 'Dickie' Rolph, even closer to the action, also found deck landing in a Skua a fraught experience. 'It was a bit of a shock to land on at a speed not far removed from the flying speed of the Swordfish,' he explained[6]. The following day, Ark took on the remaining Skuas, including 801 Squadron as *Furious* was still with the fleet in Norway, while 803 joined *Glorious*. As the carriers approached Norway they were attacked by ten Heinkels which six Skuas launched to intercept. Two Heinkels and a Dornier were destroyed though one Skua was damaged.

On the 23rd *Ark Royal* and *Glorious* arrived off Trondheim and the Skuas were immediately required to take part in fighter patrols over the ground forces at Åndalsnes and Namsos. A small number of aircraft were detached to strike seaplanes and shipping in Trondheim harbour but the weather prevented the attack until the early evening. They returned at 2000 hours, having stretched endurance to breaking point - two had to ditch before they reached the ship.

With endurance often so stretched the ships' maintainers and armourers had to be at the top of their game to get each aircraft cleared so the next could land. 'Once the Skuas landed, we'd get the guns unloaded if they had any ammo left, fold the wings, put them on the lift, get them down to the hangar, and get the lift back up again all before the next aircraft could land, as the lift left a great hole in the deck,' said 800 Squadron armourer Ron Jordan. 'We could do all that in a couple of minutes, we had it quite well worked out, though by the end there would often be two or three Skuas puffing black smoke,' – a sure sign that fuel was down to its last few drops. 'There used to be a sign, a big George Cross, and the next aircraft couldn't land until the cross was illuminated,' Jordan added[7].

An advert for Blackburn Aircraft from The Aeroplane, February 2nd 1940, depicting a Skua flying over the fleet, including HMS Ark Royal which, more than any other aircraft carrier, is associated with the Skua.

Meanwhile, Rocs from *Ark Royal* joined Sea Gladiators from *Glorious* providing combat air patrol over the fleet, which nevertheless stayed 120 miles offshore because of fears about heavy air attacks of the kind that had crippled the *Suffolk* and sunk the destroyer *Gurkha* on 9th April. Although the Rocs had been embarked, their shortcomings were apparent here as they had been in the North Sea patrols. 'We had a couple on the Ark,' confirmed 800 Squadron armourer Ron Jordan, adding 'they didn't do much flying because they were so bloody useless'[8]. Although the Roc was on paper only slightly slower than the Skua, this was with the aid of the drag cheating fairings which had to be lowered to allow the turret to revolve. As soon as this was done, and the guns swung into the slipstream, the resulting loss of speed was usually sufficient to allow even the tardiest bomber to escape.

On the same day, the army requested urgent assistance at Dombas and Otta where they were being attacked by the Luftwaffe. Six Skuas from each carrier were hastily ranged and launched. After a 220 mile flight the Skuas engaged enemy aircraft which were bombing a railway and the aerodrome at Lesjakog. Two Heinkels were shot down.

Glorious had also brought a unit of RAF Gladiators, 263 Squadron, to operate from a makeshift airfield on a frozen lake. Two Skuas escorted the fighters the 150 miles to Lake Lesjakog on the 24th, their range giving them the ability to navigate to the lake and return to the carrier. It was hoped that the Gladiators would be able to take some of the strain from the carrier aircraft in protecting ground forces, but damage and breakdowns afflicted the squadron from the start due to the harsh conditions.

On the 25th, *Ark Royal* and *Glorious* took part in Operation XD, in which the Skua squadrons were asked to concentrate on preventing bombing of Namsos and Åndalsnes. First of all though, the offensive missions planned for the previous day had to be carried out. The weather had improved enough for a more concerted attack on the military shipping at Trondheim and the many support units. Ten Skuas from *Ark Royal*'s squadrons took off at 0300 to attack in concert with Swordfish, while Skuas from *Glorious* undertook fighter patrol over Namsos and escorted the strike on Trondheim as well as dive bombing the airfield at Vaernes. At Trondheim a large transport ship was sunk and two tankers were seen to be heavily ablaze. Despite the heavy anti-aircraft fire over the target, the Skuas managed to attack some enemy aircraft in the vicinity. They claimed a Heinkel destroyed, while Finch-Noyes chased a large aircraft which eventually outran him. At Vaernes, the mixed force of Skuas and Swordfish destroyed a number of enemy aircraft and a fuel dump, and two hangars were left burning. Subsequently the Luftwaffe had to press gang Norwegian civilians to restore the airfield to operational status. In addition Norwegian sources confirmed that six seaplanes had been destroyed in Trondheim harbour.

Eight aircraft were lost, four Swordfish from enemy action and four Skuas, including all of 803 Squadron's Green section which ran out of fuel due to the distance the task force was standing offshore – a heavy total for one day. After successfully dive bombing ships in Trondheim Fjord and later shooting down a Heinkel He115, two of 803 Squadron's aircraft force-landed on the hills around Trondheim (wreckage could still be found sixty years later). The third, Lieutenant Callingham's L3048, set down almost undamaged on Spillrumstranda beach, near Namsos. The propeller's tips were bent, and the Skua was blown up on May 1st by British forces. Lieutenant Fraser-Harris, meanwhile, had suffered some bullet strikes while strafing seaplanes, but appeared to have got away with it. However, his oil line was shot through and the engine lost power and cut. Fraser-Harris ditched the Skua and he and TAG Leading Airman Russell swam for the shore. The two men were sheltered in a Norwegian farm for two days, then smuggled back to the Allied lines at Namsos, where they joined HMS *Calcutta*.

The Gladiators at Lake Lesjakog had already lost many of their number through accidents and mechanical problems, so the Skuas from *Ark Royal* and *Glorious* were still required to protect ground forces from the attentions of the Luftwaffe and support the Allies in attacking German forces. Eighteen sorties were flown on one day on 26th April, when two Heinkels were destroyed and another three damaged. 'I shot down a Heinkel over a place called Ålesund, but was shot down myself in retaliation,' said Lieutenant Filmer[9]. 'I was number two to our leader, Lieutenant William Lucy, flying in open formation up the coast when I was surprised to see three Heinkels in formation a few hundred feet above us in the opposite direction. They were travelling slowly and appeared not to have seen us, nor had Lieutenant Lucy seen them, so I waggled my wings violently to attract his attention. When he acknowledged my signal I assumed they would join me to attack the enemy but they did not do so and I was left chasing the Heinkels on my own.

'They were travelling slowly and I knew I could catch up with them and hopefully destroy at least one of them. Taking on the three was foolhardy really but I was thinking of a quick dart in and out again. I was certain that they intended to bomb Ålesund, the reason for their slowness, so I continued the chase and warned Kenneth Baldwin [Filmer's TAG] to fire if he got the chance.

'Once I caught up I kept firing at my target and watched it break away with smoke pouring out of the engine. The remaining formation turned downwards to the right. In the last few minutes shots from one of them hit my engine, rendering it useless as I broke away. I glided down and made a wheels-up landing on the water close to Ålesund harbour. To my anguish when I climbed off I found my young air gunner had been shot dead.'[10] Filmer's attack had undoubtedly saved the British and Norwegian ground forces from bombing, but the defensive weaknesses of the Skua were highlighted by this incident, and another on the same day. Petty Officer Hadley of 800 Squadron was wounded in the face, an ever present danger as the Skua's windscreen was not armoured, and the pilots often got in very close to the enemy aircraft to inflict as much damage as possible and allow the observer's machine gun to come into play. Remarkably, Hadley pressed home his attack and shot the Heinkel down, though he caused a scare to the deck crew of *Ark Royal*. 'Hadley, one pilot, got shot through the nose and another bullet in his head rest,' said armourer Ron Jordan. 'His nose swelled up, it closed his eyes, and he half crashed on landing. He skidded one way, then across, zig-zagging down the flight deck. We were all ready to leap up and unload the guns and we didn't know which way to run.'[11]

Despite the determination with which they attacked the bombers, the Skuas could not prevent considerable destruction to Åndalsnes, as by the time they reached the interception point the town was heavily on fire. They continued to patrol overhead for the rest of the day, but the damage was done.

Though the Skuas were working hard to maintain fighter patrols over the towns and armies, the large number of aircraft available to the Germans had tipped the balance in their favour. It was difficult for the aircraft from the carriers to be everywhere at once as well as providing cover for the fleet, and the Luftwaffe were increasingly able to bomb towns with impunity. The carriers had around 45 fighters between them. Before long there would be 200 German aircraft at Vaernes airfield alone.

By 27th April, none of the Gladiators at Lake Lesjakog were serviceable and once again all the fighter patrol duties fell to Skuas from the aircraft carriers off the coast. Again, a number of patrols were flown and Captain Partridge's flight, himself, Sub Lieutenant Hurle-Hobbs and Lieutenant Taylour, encountered a bomber making a run at the sloop HMS *Flamingo* which had been under heavy attack. The RN vessel was being commanded at the time by Captain J.H. Huntley, who had made several calls for air support. He later wrote: 'I didn't know I had a friend in the world... The aircraft came over the steep sides of the fjord so suddenly that I had no time to get the guns trained before they had let go and disappeared over the other side. I spent the whole day at that little game until I hadn't a bullet left, star shell, practice, the lot had gone.'[12]

After 'ten minutes at full throttle', Partridge was in range first. As he waited for the range to close the rear gunner began firing, at about 600 yards, and Partridge considered 'I was hardly within his range for accurate shooting but... he might have a lucky shot!'[13]. Partridge pressed on: 'I judged I was around 400 yards astern of him, when I opened fire with a long burst which appeared to kill his rear gunner. By this time my number two had caught up and was attacking him from underneath while I was attacking from above and from both beams'[14]. The Heinkel, riddled with bullets and one crewmember dead, began to issue smoke and lose height. However, as the Skuas turned away, Partridge's engine cut out. In 2002, when the salvaged wreck of L2940 was being examined, a bullet hole was found in the oil line of the Perseus engine – quite possibly the reason for the engine dying – the 'lucky shot' that Partridge had worried about?

Partridge and Bostock landed wheels-up by a snow covered road, fortunately behind Allied lines. After finding a hut with some provisions to install themselves in, Partridge and Bostock were unexpectedly joined by three of the crew of the downed Heinkel, and the five men spent the night in the hut under more or less friendly circumstances. Partridge and Bostock were

A postcard of Skuas dive bombing a column of fast-steaming German warships - a scenario that never took place. The markings are equally spurious, with a mix of pre-war silver and late-1940 type-A1 roundels and fin flash, together with a completely erroneous code letter on the forward fuselage. The bomb, on the other hand, is an accurate depiction of a 250lb SAP.

subsequently found by a Norwegian ski patrol and after several days restored to *Ark Royal**. In the meantime, Ned Finch-Noyes had taken temporary charge of 800 Squadron, but not before leading his Squadron mates to think he too had been lost. He finally landed on *Ark Royal* after over five hours in the air with his Skua badly shot up. He and his flight had been in the thick of the action over Åndalsnes in the afternoon. A patrol of five aircraft from 800 and 801 Squadrons intercepted two Junkers Ju88s dive bombing an army convoy. Lieutenant-Commander Bramwell and Sub-Lieutenant Wigginton followed a Junkers down into the dive and the aircraft limped away with both engines on fire. Finch-Noyes' flight pursued the other Junkers and this, too was heavily damaged. At this point, two Dornier Do17s appeared, shortly followed by a ragged formation of Heinkel He111s, fifteen aircraft in all. The Skuas split up and made separate attacks, shooting down four Heinkels in the mêlée.

The 27th April turned out to be the Skuas' most successful day during the campaign, with nine bombers confirmed destroyed and two more heavily damaged. Despite these successes, the strain of the operations was beginning to tell. *Glorious* left the theatre of operation to refuel and reinforce its squadrons with replacement aircraft.

Petty Officer H.A. 'Eric' Monk was flying fighter patrols around the area at this time, and thoroughly tested the Skua's endurance. 'Flying from Ark during Norway,' he later wrote, 'I lost my "section" and stayed over a sloop in Alesund… A He111 came over and although he kept going my Skua would not catch it… I decided after over three hours to return to *Ark Royal*. At about four hours, our endurance being four and a half hours, I began to worry although my two-hundred [gallon] tanks looked healthy still and the twenty-five gallon up forward was only used for starting. At five hours I asked to try for a bearing from Ark. Fortunately they came up and I was flying the reciprocal**. Eventually Ark came in sight. I was by now using the twenty gallons in the gravity tank. Fortunately Ark was flying off a Swordfish so I went straight in and the wires were up. After releasing the wire the engine stopped and my L2934 had to be pushed to the lift. Time for flight, five hours twenty-five minutes'. Monk had stretched the flight duration over an hour beyond the accepted limit.

The following day a further attack on Vaernes aerodrome took place. Many enemy aircraft were destroyed on the ground and the Skuas shot down a further five in the air. Gallagher, Spurway and Rooper carried out a dive-bombing attack on transport ships in Trondheim harbour. The Skuas scored at least one hit on one ship with a 250lb bomb, and further attacks were made on seaplanes with 'Cooper' bombs. However, Midshipman Gallagher found himself separated from his section and unable to find *Ark Royal*. Returning to the coast, the pilot force landed at Setnesmoen airfield, near Åndalsnes. The story has since passed into legend. Gallagher camouflaged his aircraft and refuelled the machine from the wrecked Gladiators of 263 Squadron which had been abandoned. 'He got some petrol out of some RAF aircraft, and I'm not sure he didn't even get some

---

*   A full description of this incident is provided in Major Partridge's book *Operation Skua* published by the Fleet Air Arm Museum, Yeovilton, 1983

**   This meant Monk was flying directly towards Ark Royal, on the opposite course ('reciprocal') to the bearing that had been provided by the ship. Monk was lucky – aircraft carriers during war time did not often break radio silence to give bearings to pilots

from motor cars that the Norwegians gave him', added Gallagher's friend and fellow 800 Squadron pilot Midshipman Derek Martin[15]. He found the Army HQ in Åndalsnes and sent a request to *Ark Royal* to drop a box of Coffman cartridges. However, before this could be done the Naval Liaison Officer informed Gallagher that he would have to destroy the Skua if the aircraft could not be started. However, 'with the aircraft's destruction in view, I was stripping it of all moveable gear when I discovered five starter cartridges,' Gallagher noted in his combat report. The exact truth of this miraculous discovery is slightly unclear, as other accounts suggest that Gallagher found the starters in a crashed Skua when faced with the destruction of his aircraft. However the cartridges were acquired, Gallagher and his TAG were on their way as soon as dawn on the morning of the 30th offered enough light – not before they had been strafed by a Heinkel. 'I set course for Lerwick, then Hatston' Gallagher's report blandly states[16]. This says nothing of the supreme feat of navigation and nerve that got Gallagher and his TAG back to Orkney. 'We didn't have any maps of Norway so I heard he tore the map off the wall of a school,' explained Derek Martin. 'He took off and flew due west until he'd gone as far as he thought he needed then turned south and luckily came across the Orkney islands or possibly the Shetlands, for which he got the DFC'.

On 29th April several attacks on the fleet took place, but the fighters were able to ensure that none got through to seriously threaten the ships. Four bombers were shot down by 800, 803 and 801 in addition to one claimed by *Ark Royal*'s anti-aircraft gunners. With *Glorious* back from refuelling, *Ark Royal* withdrew to the Faeroe Islands to give the pilots a rest.

When *Ark Royal* returned at the end of the month the Luftwaffe had switched to high level attacks, above the useful ceiling of the Skuas – in part an acknowledgement of the increasing effectiveness of the fighters. With the experience built up over the short time in Norway, the three squadrons learned to play to the Skua's strengths and mitigate the weaknesses somewhat. By using the aircraft's endurance and economical cruise, patrolling Skuas could use cloud cover and loiter at altitude, diving on bombers whenever they appeared. However, with the onset of summer, less cloud cover and the change in German tactics the aircrews were less effective against the

An advert for Blackburn aircraft from Flight magazine in December 1943. By this date the Skua had been out of service for over two years, but Blackburn was clearly proud of the aircraft's achievements. It is shown dive bombing German supply ships during the Norwegian campaign of 1940.

bombers. Nevertheless, higher level bombing reduced accuracy further (the Luftwaffe did not have an effective high-level bomb sight) and if less damage was done to the Luftwaffe, they were also inflicting less. Attacks by Stukas were rarer too, but one of the Ju87s was shot down on the 1st of May when a Skua followed the bombers into a dive.

Central Norway was now being evacuated, and the Skuas were required to cover the withdrawal. Fortunately, Åndalsnes and Namsos were cleared of Allied troops without coming under serious attack. This phase of the fighting was drawing to a close, but the Allies planned to mount concerted operations in northern Norway where resistance to the invasion had been stiffer and the German forces had a less secure foothold.

Ark Royal and *Glorious* returned to Orkney, where the ships were replenished and several aircrews given up for lost returned to their squadrons, including Midshipman Gallagher.

On 6th May, *Ark Royal* arrived off Narvik with 800, 803, and 801 Squadrons, while in northern Norway, British and Norwegian forces had been preparing airfields for RAF fighters having learned many of the lessons from Lake Lesjakog. For the next week, the Skua squadrons maintained patrols and escorted reconnaissance and strike missions. On the 8th, the fighters 'bounced' a flight of seaplanes in Beisfjord and shot down two of them, but Lieutenant Charlton in Skua L2916 was forced down on the beach at Tovik, near Harstad, after a battle with a Dornier Do26 during which his engine cut out. Charlton had an eventful time trying to rejoin his squadron. He walked to Allied lines and joined the Polish transport MS *Chrobry* which was carrying soldiers to bolster forces south of Narvik which were trying to resist the German advance. However, the ship was sunk by Stukas and the pilot had to be picked up by a destroyer before he could be reunited with 803 Squadron.

On 9th May Lieutenant Lucy and Captain Partridge of 800 Squadron were awarded the Distinguished Service Order for the strike on the *Königsberg*, with all the other crews mentioned in despatches. On the same day, 806 Squadron carried out its first offensive mission with a raid to attack a ship, which according to reports was potentially a cruiser, at Doksjeir jetty in Bergen harbour. The eight Skuas, escorted by six Blenheim MkIVFs of 254 Squadron Coastal Command, dived through the low cloud base and immediately aimed for the ship, now thought to be a transport. Several hits were claimed and the Skuas escaped without damage, although one of the Blenheims crashed into the harbour. Complete surprise had been achieved and the two officers leading the raid, Evans and his

A graphic depiction of the sinking of the cruiser Königsberg by Skuas in April 1940. Blackburn Aircraft were not reticent in using the mission to publicise their aircraft and commissioned at least two illustrations of the attack for use in advertisements. This is from Flight in September 1940.

Observer Lieutenant Vicent-Jones, were awarded the DSC, while Petty Officers Muskett and Clare were awarded the DSM. The raid was swiftly followed up with another on the 11th, this time aimed at the oil fuel tanks at Bergen. Again, complete surprise was achieved and the six Skuas dive bombed the tanks before any anti-aircraft fire could begin. The attack was carried out very skilfully, particularly for a new squadron, and within a minute and a half the two largest tanks were heavily aflame and the Skuas were on their way home. On the following day the squadron again flew from Hatston to Bergen to attack a transport ship which was believed to be carrying anti-aircraft guns to reinforce the port's defences. Unfortunately the squadron was not used to attacking moving targets and all bombs fell astern of the ship.

On the 13th, Allied forces led by the French Foreign Legion stormed the beaches at Narvik. This was the first opposed landing on an enemy shore of the war, and the Skuas undertook close support work. A great deal was learned during the assault on Narvik, not least that air support was critical to keep the enemy pinned down and make gaps in the lines that the landing troops could force their way through. Above all, it proved that a heavily defended coast could be successfully overrun and began the learning that would lead to the North Africa and Normandy landings.

However, word reached the fleet on the 14th that the Netherlands had fallen, leaving the continued operations in Norway on less certain footing. Later that day came what was, for the local forces, a still greater blow. Lieutenant Bill Lucy, Officer Commanding 803 Squadron, was shot down and killed while defending the fleet against a bombing attack. His flight had intercepted five bombers at 18,000ft, close to the maximum height the Skuas could operate at. One bomber was damaged and the others scattered, diving to sea level to try and escape. This was not the best way to avoid Skuas which could dive with the best and Lucy attempted to press the advantage. As his combat reports revealed, Lucy had no reservations about closing to point blank range to make the most of the four Brownings. Smoke burst from the Heinkel's port engine and Lucy's Skua started to turn away, possibly to give Observer Mike Hanson a shot. At this point, according to some reports the aircraft was seen to explode just above the sea, and aircraft searching the spot reported seeing only the tail floating in the sea – of Lucy and Hanson there was no sign. Gray and Clayton took so much time looking for the missing airmen that they ran dangerously short on fuel and had to land at Breivikstranda.

In addition to his DSO Lucy was also confirmed an ace with seven victories, the only ace to score all his victories on the Skua. With his contribution to the Konigsberg raid and extensive air combat, Lucy was one of the personnel who did most to turn the Skua into an effective weapon. The destruction of two Junkers Ju87s that day was scant consolation.

At this time of year, as far north as the fleet was stationed, there was barely any darkness, which put added pressure on the aircrews, anti-aircraft gunners and machinery. Operations continued more or less round the clock and some of the aircrews had spent only two nights in harbour since they embarked. The Luftwaffe was also increasing in strength and many more fighters were available. On the 15th, while the unfortunate Charlton was busy being bombed on the *Chrobry*, a number of Skua missions took place. While escorting a strike,

Skuas of 803 Squadron engaged German bombers and Petty Officer A.G Johnson was wounded by a bullet that entered the cockpit through the windscreen and passed through his shoulder, finally lodging in the seat. His TAG, Leading Airman Coston, was wounded in the face by splinters. Once again skill and experience combined with the Skua's deck landing qualities allowed a wounded pilot to recover to *Ark Royal*, though Johnson was out of action for the next three months convalescing.

On 16th May, Harris and Glover bounced a flight of twin-engined aircraft which, with their slim fuselage and twin tails, the Skuas took for Dornier Do17s. In fact they were Messerschmitt Bf110s of Kampfgruppe 30, and the Skuas desperately tried to outmanoeuvre the four fighters. One of the Messerschmitts shot down Harris. 'A bullet splattered through my windscreen and into my shoulder after several head-on attacks and I parked in a fjord off Narvik. The Skua, sedate to the end, waddled to the sea bed' Harris later wrote. He and his Observer were later picked up by a RN destroyer. Glover and his TAG Wright, still in the fight, shot down another of the fighters and escaped. A patrol from 800 and 803 squadrons consisting of a flight from each happened on some Junkers Ju88 fighters from the same unit as the Messerschmitts and fared better. Each flight shot down a Junkers for no loss.

The Skua was, on paper, no match for the German fighters. The Messerschmitt Bf110 could reach 297mph at sea level, some 70mph faster than the Skua, and was armed with four machine guns and two cannon. In practice, the German machine was unwieldy and not suited to dogfighting. Even the Ju88 fighters were considerably faster and better armed than a Skua, although they were really only suitable in the night fighter role, being too big and clumsy to dogfight. The Skua was stressed for dive bombing and this meant it could be manoeuvred more violently. The Bf109 was a different proposition and rather more agile than its stable mate. Even so, the Skua crews had a few tricks up their sleeve. The flaps that made it such a successful dive bomber could be used to facilitate a rapid change in direction in a turn or throw the aircraft bodily upwards when flying straight. This was enough to put any pursuing fighter off its aim, and even allowed the Skua pilot a chance to shoot back, though in reality the ruse could only buy time until the Bf109s ran short on fuel or the Skuas found some cloud to hide in. A variation on this technique would be rediscovered by Sea Harrier pilots during the Falklands conflict in 1982. 'Viffing' (after Vector In Forward Flight) involved swinging the Harrier's thrust-vectoring jet nozzles forward rather than using the flaps to effect a sudden change in speed and direction.

On the 16th May, 806 Squadron carried out another raid from Hatston to attack a warship which had been reported in Bergen harbour. However, the Skuas could not locate this vessel so made for the secondary target of the fuel tanks at Skaalevik. Unlike all the previous missions, the escorting Blenheims of 254 Squadron failed to make contact so the Skuas proceeded alone. They reached the target, over which a large cloud provided welcome cover, and dived on the tanks with 250lb bombs and 20lb Cooper bombs. The tanks were left thoroughly on fire, but the squadron had noticed considerably heavier anti-aircraft defences than on previous missions. Perhaps the vessel that had escaped on the 12th had indeed been carrying extra guns.

After these exchanges the weather closed in for several days, but so did the German ground forces, which had reached Mo. Still, the Allies were about to receive reinforcements. *Glorious* and *Furious* arrived on the 20th May, bringing with them more RAF fighters. Bardufoss was a much better base of operations for the re-equipped 263 Squadron than Lake Lesjakog, and the conditions at this time of year were more favourable for operating from a temporary airstrip.

Sadly, the writing was on the wall for the Norwegian campaign as the situation in France was dire, and in Norway Allied troops were retreating to Bodø. In fact, the order to evacuate Norway was received on 24th May but the local commanders decided to continue with plans to capture Narvik temporarily in order to wreck the iron ore and transport facilities. To help achieve this, *Glorious* brought 46 Squadron's Hurricanes to reinforce the Gladiators and these immediately made their presence felt, giving the Luftwaffe a much harder time locally than the FAA had been able to manage. They took the pressure off so much that *Ark Royal* was able to disengage and return to the Clyde on the 27th May to refuel and re-arm. The following day Narvik was captured, but would be held only as long as was necessary to deny German forces strategically valuable resources.

Sure enough, the evacuation began early in June. On 5th June two speculative raids were flown with Swordfish and Skuas to reconnoitre and bomb any targets they saw. Operation 'Alphabet' began on the 8th and the two Skua squadrons were in action flying round the clock patrols over the troops, fleet and convoys. Lt. Commander Derek Martin described one such mission: 'We were mainly supporting naval activities and any army activities, so we were flying CAPs [Combat Air Patrols] above wherever the fleet happened to be. We were flying those every day, and sometimes twice a day. Occasionally we would see a German Heinkel, a floatplane, and do a bit of chasing. I was never attacked by a German fighter – none of us were'. Even so, such activity was not without risk. 'On one occasion when I was chasing after a German floatplane I suddenly found myself surrounded by flak' – which turned out to be from an RN destroyer! Fortunately on this occasion the flak was inaccurate and Martin escaped without harm. The Skuas were also required to strafe German forces to stem their advance from the south. 'We saw a couple of tanks and some lorries moving slowly northwards,' wrote Lieutenant Commander John Casson of 803 Squadron. 'We radioed the position to the Ark and then in line astern we dived down on them and opened up with our front guns and dropped a few 20lb bombs'. Meanwhile, strike missions continued.

'Before the *Scharnhorst* we'd done one dive bombing raid on a radio station,' said Naval Airman L.G. Richards. 'It didn't work out too well, the weather was very bad. I saw what looked like whisps of straw going past which I realised were tracer bullets. I was rather in disgust that someone was shooting at me! I tried to shoot back but couldn't align the gun.'[17]

The evacuation was proceeding well, but on the 8th, disaster struck. *Glorious*, having been detached to proceed to Scapa independently escorted by the destroyers *Ardent* and *Acasta*, was caught by the German battlecruisers *Scharnhorst* and *Gneisenau*. Despite a determined attack by the two destroyers, all three ships were sunk with the loss of over a thousand men and the 46 Squadron

Hurricanes, which had succeeded in landing on the carrier despite a complete lack of deck training, and no aircraft carrier equipment.

Scharnhorst had however been damaged by a torpedo launched by *Acasta*, and had to put into Trondheim for repairs. Following RAF photo reconnaissance which had identified the presence of German heavy units in Trondheim, *Ark Royal* was ordered by the Admiralty and Admiral Wells to prepare every available aircraft for a strike. The original plan called for 21 Skuas and 22 Swordfish (more aircraft than *Ark* had available), but at some point this complement was whittled down to fifteen Skuas. Over 60 years later, it is difficult to see how the raid was allowed to take place. The War Cabinet and Air Staff felt that Skuas and Swordfish would have little chance against the many fighter aircraft which were known to be in the area and Churchill himself questioned the wisdom of the plan. Cabinet Office minutes from 10th June state 'the Prime Minister expressed grave doubts as to the wisdom of the operation… It would be a gallant operation, but one which, in his opinion, might prove far too costly'.[18] Naval Air Division at the Admiralty counselled that losses could be expected to be high while chances of success were slim, and tried to persuade the Commander in Chief of the Norway Campaign Task Force to send as large a force as possible. Daylight was virtually constant at this time of year so a dawn raid in the manner of the Bergen strike would not be possible. Furthermore Trondheim was further inland which would give more warning of the raid, the port was very well defended with anti-aircraft fire and Vaernes airfield's 80 fighters a few miles away. To give the Skuas some chance of success, a bombing raid on

The remarkable discovery of Lieutenant-Commander John Casson's Skua was achieved by a team on the survey ship SV Gunnerus, including NTNU students, and was led by Torkell Nodland and Klas Gjolmesli. This image shows the Skua sitting upright on the bottom of the fjord in 242 metres of water. (Torkell Nodland, via Klas Gjolmesli)

Vaernes by seven Coastal Command Bristol Beauforts was planned to keep the fighters from intercepting the Skuas. In addition, the RAF was to send Bristol Blenheims from 254 Squadron to cover the dive bombers over the target.

Fifteen aircraft and crews from 800 and 803 Squadrons were prepared – several of the crews had never dive-bombed before, despite Admiral Wells' later claim that the fifteen pilots were chosen because they had prior experience. In fact, Lieutenant Commander John Casson, commanding 803 Squadron, who would technically be leading the raid, admitted to having 'little or no' experience of dive bombing at all! Some pilots had very little time on the Skua and both squadron commanders were sure the raid would lead to heavy casualties and many of the crews felt they might not return, so the atmosphere the evening before the raid was subdued.

The beginning of the raid was not auspicious. Captain Partridge managed to nearly throw his armourer into the sea! Ron Jordan, the armourer in question said: 'I used to have to stand by Captain Partridge's plane alongside Lieutenant Bostock in case he needed any last minute alterations. He asked me to get two aluminium sea markers. Meanwhile Captain Partridge was doing his engine tests and I don't think he knew I was back. He revved the engine right up, and the blast from the propeller took me horizontal! I thought I was going to go over the back'. Fortunately for Jordan, his grip on the Skua was sufficient. The sea-markers were usually quite innocuous devices, used to aid navigation. 'It was a big tin filled with aluminium filings,' explained Jordan. 'When it hit the sea it would spread out with a big radius, then when you saw it on the way back you knew you were in the right place to change course. You could rely on

The warships at Trondheim, photographed by Lieutenant Spurway's Telegraphist Air Gunner Petty Officer Hart, during the attack. In addition to Scharnhorst, the heavy cruiser Admiral Hipper and several destroyers were present. (National Archives)

The Scharnhorst (A) and a destroyer (D) off Trondheim, taken as 800 Squadron are about to start their attack run. (National Archives)

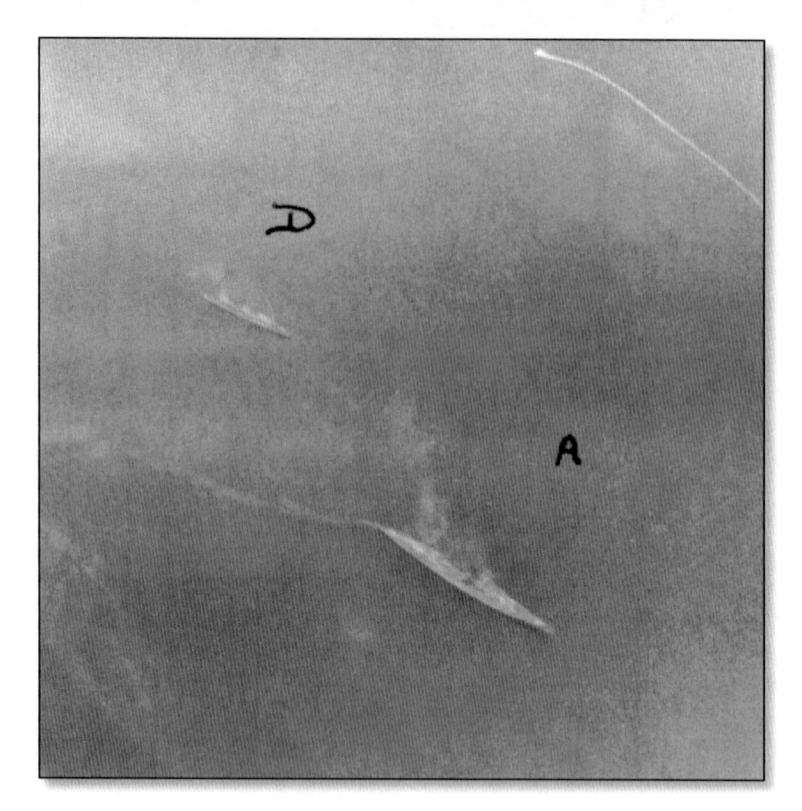

the marker staying in more or less the same place.' However, Jordan harbours suspicions that Bostock might have had quite another use in mind for the markers – one which hints at just how desperate the men were feeling. 'It was to let them out into his slipstream to blanket the windscreen of the Me109 sitting on his tail!' Jordan suggested[19].

Five minutes after midnight on 13th June, the fifteen Skuas took off from *Ark Royal* and climbed to 12,000ft. It was full daylight by the time the squadrons took off as there was no darkness at this time of year, only a brief 'dusk' at the nadir before the sun began to rise again. The 15 Skuas crossed the coast in brilliant sunshine, fifty miles from the target. 'It was going to be the sort of day when flying would be sheer bliss, except that the one thing we all wanted was a nice overcast day,' said Casson. 'The enemy would see us coming with all the time they wanted to get ready for us'. The Blenheims from 254 Squadron failed to arrive on time due to an error in calculating the range, and with time running short 800 and 803 Squadrons left the rendezvous and headed for Trondheim. Though this was a blow, the Blenheim MkIVF was barely faster than the Skuas and in essence a light bomber.

In the van was 803 Squadron, led by Casson, in three flights of three. Following was 800 Squadron, led by Partridge, in two flights of three. The two squadrons divided to make separate attacks, and entered a shallow dive to pick up speed over the target. However, the RAF Beauforts (of which only four reached the target) had completed the raid on Vaernes, which was over by the time the Skuas arrived – minimal damage had been inflicted and fighters which were airborne to defend the airfield were perfectly placed to descend on the dive bombers even before they reached Trondheim. 'We had flown over an island which was about 70 or 80 miles offshore so we were seen clearly by the Germans and they had plenty of warning,' said Derek Martin, who was flying in the final section of 800 Squadron. 'The support there was supposed to be from RAF Blenheims and Beauforts never worked out and we ran into a hell of a shower of fighters – Me109s and 110s. The flight I was in was Tail End Charlie and they picked us off one by one. We were still around ten miles from the target.' Martin's flight had been 'bounced' by Bf110s approaching unseen from the dark flanks of the mountains, and before they knew what had hit them they were in serious trouble.

As the Skuas barrelled towards the harbour at 240kts the planned attack was already coming apart at the seams. Martin's section was all shot down. Midshipman Gallagher and Petty Officer Crawford were both killed after Messerschmitt Bf109s repeatedly attacked the Skua and it crashed into trees near Tempelet, Hermstadheia. 'Gallagher's aircraft was found with the pilot, gunner and bomb all lying beside a wrecked aircraft so he didn't have a chance,' said Martin. Martin bailed out when enemy bullets entering under his seat destroyed his control column. 'I immediately lost control of wing and tail plane surfaces and the aircraft went into an increasingly steep dive. With incendiary smoke coming from under my seat I shouted to "jump" three times into the Gosport tube to Tremeer, my TAG, before opening the hood – I then abandoned the aircraft.' Sadly, Leading Airman W.J. Tremeer had been killed by the gunfire that took away the controls.

Lieutenant 'Ned' Finch-Noyes was next, set upon by two Bf110s in a 'scissor' attack. The pilot was killed by a volley of bullets from an attacking fighter. Cunningham had time to bail out but was lucky to escape the wrecked aircraft.

The crashed Skua, L2955, flown by Sub-Lieutenant Bartlett and Naval Airman Richards following the raid against the Scharnhorst on 13th June 1940. The Skua was damaged by German fighters and Bartlett crashed in a field south of Trondheim. The crew set fore to the aircraft before being taken prisoner. (via Øyvind Lamo)

The view of Trondheim from the rear of Lieutenant Spurway and Petty Officer Hart's Skua after the raid, as the few surviving aircraft escaped. The smoke on the shore was caused by the unsuccessful diversionary raid by RAF Bristol Beauforts which only served to put the defences on their guard before the Skuas arrived. (National Archives)

Monk's TAG, Petty Officer 'Dickie' Rolph, saw Cunningham ensnared in the Skua's W/T aerial as he tried to bail out (recounted after Dickie's death by his brother, Denis, to whom the TAG had described the events of 13th June) before freeing himself, only to discover his parachute was damaged by gunfire. Fortunately the parachute stayed intact long enough for Cunningham to make a safe landing.

Monk and Rolph did not escape the attentions of the fighters for long. A Messerschmitt Bf110 attacked their aircraft and, recognising that there was no hope of making the target, Monk jettisoned the bomb and played the Skua pilot's trump card. '... put down flaps and turned sharply to port,' says Monk's combat report after the attack. The Messerschmitt attacked six times and with each attack the Messerschmitt was made to overshoot and Monk was even able to get on its tail and fire off a few bursts. This was no mistake. 'Dickie and Monk were both Petty Officers and messed together,' said Denis. 'Dickie and Monk spent a lot of time together and they were always discussing what to do if they were attacked.' When the Bf110 came in to attack, Rolph would give the signal and Monk would use the throttle and flaps to 'park' the aircraft and make the Messerschmitt zoom past. Eventually the Bf110, after making its final attack from a distant 1,000 yards, broke off - 'I suppose he must have run out of ammunition,' said Denis. Rolph and Monk comprised the only all-Petty Officer crew in the squadron. While other crews were made up entirely of officers, several were made up of officers and enlisted men, and the traditional aloofness between the ranks must have made communication more problematic.

Of 800 Squadron, only Captain Partridge and his Observer Lieutenant Bostock, Lieutenant Spurway and TAG Petty Officer Hart made it to the target area. 'Intense anti-aircraft fire of every type was encountered, both from ships and shore,' said Spurway in his combat report. The fliers were dismayed to see that in addition to the battlecruiser, the heavy cruiser *Admiral Hipper*, another

The remains of the first Skua to be shot down on the raid on the Scharnhorst on June 13th 1940. Midshipman Gallagher and Petty Officer Crawford were both killed after their flight was bounced by Messerschmitt Bf 110s. (via Øyvind Lamo)

cruiser and a destroyer were anchored in the fjord, each firing a fierce volume of flak. 'The tracer bullets commenced rising well before we were within striking distance,' remarked Cecil Filmer who was flying with 803 Squadron. 'Unexpectedly, there was a grim beauty about them'[20].

803 Squadron in the van had so far escaped the fighters which had attacked the rear of 800 Squadron's formation, but not for long. Filmer noted: 'the trouble

Another picture of Lieutenant Commander John Casson's Skua. The serial is not known, but the aircraft is in remarkable condition even down to the glazing being intact and the colour scheme still apparent. The aircraft was discovered on the 25th April 2007(Torkell Nodland, via Klas Gjolmesli)

was we had to cope with the enemy fighters, 110s and 109s. We were attacked as we were coming in; they were waiting for us when we got there.[21]'

Casson led his squadron into the dive from 5,000ft from the direction of the battlecruiser's bow, into a storm of AA fire. 'For a moment I thought I was seeing "liver spots"', said Casson. 'It was tracer flak. It was exactly like flying in a hailstorm with the projectiles flying up'[22]. Lieutenant Gibson in the rear of the formation took his flight in the opposite direction. 'It was not worth while to expose my aircraft to an extra five minutes of anti-aircraft fire' he said, 'we attacked from stern to bow being in a perfect position to do so'[23]. Despite the flak and fighters, the pilots were still determined to get their bombs on target. 'I used the same tactics as when attacking the *Königsberg*,' said Lieutenant Filmer, 'so might have hit. I went in at the same angle, 60° which suited me very well. There were reports of only one bomb hitting and that was a dud. I hope mine hit, even if it was a dud'.

The squadron was even attacked by fighters in the midst of the flak as they dive-bombed. 'I myself was subjected to a poor spirited attack by the Me 109s when in my dive,' said Gibson, adding 'one Me 109 was driven off by the Skua it attacked'.

Meanwhile, Partridge led the remaining two aircraft of 800 Squadron round to the stern of the ship and into a steep dive from 7,000ft, giving them the best chance of an accurate bomb run but making them agonisingly open to fighter attack. Lieutenant Spurway, following Partridge down, saw one bomb near-miss off the starboard quarter and then a bright flash just aft of the funnel.

The squadrons had been splintered by the repeated attacks and it was now every man for himself. Some of the Skuas escaped by continuing their dives to sea level and sneaking away along the coast.

Meanwhile, Finch-Noyes' TAG Petty Officer Cunningham had been taken prisoner. During interrogation it was put to him that he had flown from *Ark Royal*. He is reported to have answered 'don't be bloody silly, you sank the *Ark Royal* last year, don't you remember?'[24].

Casson and Fanshawe were forced down near Kjora, Geitastrand, after a spirited but fruitless attempt to escape from a Messerschmitt Bf109. 'There is an aerobatic manoeuvre called a "flick roll"', said Casson. 'On that morning I did it accidentally by turning too tightly and we were at 300 feet... I heard a plaintive bleat from the back cockpit, "Jesus Christ!"'[25] Casson put his damaged Skua down in the fjord and he and Fanshawe were taken prisoner.

Partridge and Bostock were caught by two Bf109s and crashed in the sea by the island of Bessholmen. They survived several attacks, but against two aircraft there was little they could do, and when the Bf109s attacked simultaneously from astern and abeam, Bostock was killed and Partridge bailed out after suffering burns. Sub-Lieutenant R.E. Bartlett and Naval Airman L.G. Richards force landed after a terrifying, barely-controlled flight from the target. 'We went down and down and down,' said TAG Lloyd Richards, unbeknownst to whom at the time, Bartlett had been wounded. 'I think he was nearly gone,' said Richards. 'He blacked out and when he came to we were flying low over trees, very low. The aircraft was all over the place. We shouldn't have survived that'[26]. In the confusion, or in trying to avoid fighters, Bartlett had flown miles south of Trondheim, away from *Ark Royal*. Filmer and McKee were pursued by two Messerschmitt Bf110s. 'All I could immediately think of was to try to deceive them by putting on port rudder and keeping the wings level to cause us to skid as we flew and so upset their aim,' he recalled. Then McKee was hit and for Filmer, enough was enough. He put the Skua down on the sea close to Frøsetskjæret, where both men were captured. Harris and Stevenson, in Skua L2992, crashed into the hillside above the farm at Kjøra. The two aircrew were brought to Orkdal hospital, but Harris died just after arrival. Naval Airman Stevenson died at the hospital a year later on 31st May 1941.

As the seven remaining aircraft made their way back to *Ark Royal*, some pilots asked for a D/F bearing from the carrier. This was unusual as a broadcast from the ship could give away its position to the enemy - in fact the aircrews had been told that they could radio their call-sign once for a D/F bearing, quite a concession particularly so soon after the loss of *Glorious*. However, as the Skuas returned, *Ark Royal* did not break radio silence and the crews were forced to navigate back by taking a fix using the ship's revolving beacon, which was quite a feat of navigation for a TAG not trained in formal navigation. Just after the surviving aircraft made it back to *Ark Royal* the carrier sailed into a patch of fog, meaning any last stragglers would have had no chance of finding the ship. A report to the Cabinet largely blamed the fog for the heavy losses. In fact, there were no more Skuas to find their way back.

The raid had caused no damage to *Scharnhorst*. Due to the withering defensive fire the bombing had not been nearly as accurate as on previous raids and, while one bomb did hit the warship amidships, it failed to explode. RAF documents reveal how to penetrate the *Scharnhorst*'s horizontal armour, a 2,000lb bomb dropped at 6,800ft would be the minimum necessary, and noted that 500lb SAP bombs could not penetrate *Scharnhorst*'s armour from any height. It would not have been impossible for a properly planned and executed raid by Skuas to have done some damage to the ship's upperworks and kept it in port for longer – a tactic used in Operation Tungsten in 1944, the successful strike against the *Tirpitz*. However, there were too few Skuas with too little cover facing too much opposition and with inadequate coordination. At best the raid was a waste of men and aircraft and at worst it could be argued that dive bombing in the RN never really recovered. As Partridge and Casson had been captured, Lieutenant R.M. Smeeton and Lieutenant J.M. Bruen took over 800 and 803 Squadrons respectively. The loss of two squadron commanders, particularly the experienced and battle-hardened Partridge, was a savage blow to the Fleet Air Arm. 'That raid was the ultimate blunder of the Norwegian campaign,' said Derek Martin. 'The penultimate and far more catastrophic blunder was the detaching of *Glorious* and the two destroyers from the fleet to proceed independently to Scapa for a non-operational reason: the sinking of those ships with the loss of over 1,500 lives – and yet to be fully explained – was the cause of the Trondheim disaster.' Few would disagree. The raid had indeed done nothing to mitigate or avenge the earlier tragedy and had merely compounded the loss.

The Norwegian campaign is regarded as a disaster, but the effort was not entirely wasted. Much erroneous pre-war thinking was (painfully) debunked during those three months, and for the first time there was a hint that the Luftwaffe might not be as invincible as the pre-war hype suggested. It lost 260 aircraft compared with 126 Allied aircraft, (though a further 43 sank with *Glorious*). The Allies scored at rate of 2:1, and even allowing for accidents, this was a genuine success against the well equipped and confident German air force. Other improvements had been made, necessity causing the sometimes over-rigid structure of the Royal Navy to bend somewhat. Experienced rating pilots such as 803 Squadron's Petty Officer A.G. 'Johnno' Johnson and 800 Squadron's Petty Officer H.A. 'Eric' Monk being made flight commanders ahead of (less experienced) officers – possibly the first time ratings had led officers into battle in RN history!

---

1. Dickie Rolph BEM, article 'The Konigsberg Story' in the magazine of the TAGs Association, by kind permission
2. Letter from C.H. Filmer to the author 10th December 2006
3. Letter from Commander G. Hare to Major R.T. Partridge 28th February 1984, reproduced by kind permission of Simon Partridge
4. Historical Section Naval Staff, Naval Operations of the Campaign in Norway, p.26
5. William Jameson, Ark Royal, p.90
6. R.S. Rolph BEM, unpublished memoir That First Phoney Year
7. Ron Jordan, in conversation with the author, 21st November 2006
8. Ron Jordan, in conversation with the author, 21st November 2006
9. C.H. Filmer in conversation with the author 11th November 2006
10. Letter from C.H. Filmer to the author 10th December 2006
11. Ron Jordan, in conversation with the author, 21st November 2006
12. Captain J.H Hartley, letter to Major R.T. Partridge, 13th September 1974. Reproduced by kind permission of Simon Partridge. In a strange twist of fate, the Flamingo, which survived the war, was later sold to West Germany and named the Graf Spee
13. R.T. Partridge, 'Operation Skua', p. 69
14. Unnamed report by Major R.T. Partridge reproduced by kind permission of Simon Partridge
15. Derek Martin in conversation with the author 5th November 2006
16. Documents from the National Archives under ADM 199/480
17. L.G. Richards, in conversation with the author January 2007
18. Cabinet Office minutes from the National Archives, under CAB/65/13
19. Ron Jordan in conversation with Simon Partridge, reproduced by kind permission
20. Letter from C.H. Filmer to Øyvind Lamo, reproduced by kind permission
21. C.H. Filmer in conversation with the author 11th November 2006
22. John Casson, unpublished memoir reproduced by kind permission
23. Documents from the National Archives under ADM 199/480
24. Kenneth Poolman, Ark Royal, p.117
25. John Casson, unpublished memoire
26. L.G. Richards in conversation with the author at the Blackburn Skua crew reunion, Fleet Air Arm Museum, Yeovilton, October 2006

Dunkirk and the Channel

The second fighter patrol of the day was flown by Fleet Air Arm dive bombers and two-seater fighters. "The 37 Skuas and Rocs were a splendid sight as they took off in mass formation," recalled Clarke. "They looked a bit more operational than some of the others even if their maximum speed was only 225mph. They came back just before lunchtime, so I stayed to watch them land. There were not many; I counted six; where were the others? One belly-flopped and I went across to see what had happened, the blood-wagon passing me on the way. That aircraft was a complete write-off. Bullets and cannon shells had ripped the fuselage from end to end - the after cockpit was sprayed liberally with blood, the inside of the glasshouse reddened throughout by the forward draft The front cockpit, if anything, was worse. Two bullet holes through the back of the pilot's seat showed where he had been hit, and his parachute, still in position, was saturated with blood. The instrument panel was shattered wreckage, and on the floor was a boot - and the remains of a foot. I was nearly sick with the horror of it. How that pilot flew home will never be known, for I found he was dead when they dragged him out. Of those 37 Skuas and Rocs, only nine came back; of the nine, only four were serviceable." This account from Alexander McKee's 'Strike From The Sky' depicts Skuas and Rocs at Dunkirk as expendable and torn to shreds by a vastly superior Luftwaffe.

Blackburn Roc L3105 'L6R' in flight. This aircraft belonged to 806 Squadron which was the fourth front line Skua/Roc squadron to form. L6 is 806 Squadron's code, with 'L' referring to the fact that the squadron was part of HMS Illustrious' air group. Rocs from 806 took part in operations over Dunkirk and the English Channel in 1940. The aircraft carries bomb racks. (Fleet Air Arm Museum)

The difficult job of entering the Roc's turret. In addition to the normal manner of entry, as seen here facilitated by sliding panels in the turret glazing, an escape hatch was fitted in the floor. Note the spring-loaded steps in the side of the fuselage, and how little room there appears to be for entry and exit. (BAE Systems)

The truth is somewhat different. Two Skua and Roc squadrons operated over Dunkirk and had a hard time during the evacuation – as did the RAF, the army and the Navy - but nevertheless gave a markedly better account of themselves than McKee's wildly exaggerated (if not completely fabricated) account suggests. While Dowding was hoarding many of his Spitfires and Hurricanes in readiness for the Battle of Britain, the evacuation of troops had to be covered, and the shortfall left by an overstretched Fighter Command had to be made up. The Wehrmacht, supported devastatingly effectively by the Luftwaffe, had swept across France and in less than a month had the British army cornered. The Luftwaffe had to be prevented from helping the army tear through the last line of defence and Coastal Command was required to bolster the air support with any aircraft it could muster. Several Fleet Air Arm squadrons were put under the auspices of Coastal Command, including 801 and 806 which moved from Hatston to Detling and Manston in Kent. They were joined by a squadron of Albacores (new aircraft seeing their first action) and four squadrons of Swordfish, as well as a rag-tag collection of aircraft from Anti-Aircraft Co-operation, Air-Sea Rescue and Maintenance units, including at least one more Skua which had been used by the RAF as a target tug.

On 28th May, the evacuation had started in earnest. Reichsmarshall Göring committed the Luftwaffe to destroying the remainder of the BEF and on this day the skies were swarming with German aircraft. On their first fighter patrol over the Channel, 806 Squadron were set upon by RAF Spitfires, who shot down Lieutenant Campbell-Horsfall (who lost a finger as a result) and left Midshipman Hogg's aircraft to limp back to Manston where it crashed on landing.

Naval Airman Burton, Hogg's TAG, was killed*. Aircraft recognition was poor on both sides at this time, and the Skua would have been largely unfamiliar to both the RAF and the Armée de l'Air. Moreover, the Fleet Air Arm's camouflage at that time bore some resemblance to that worn by the Luftwaffe's fighters. It was perhaps for this reason that modifications to the colours later appeared, with the upper camouflage demarcation line being extended down to the level of the wing from the rear of the cowling to the front of the tail fin. To compound the problem, inter-service communication appears to have been poor. Several Allied aircraft were shot down by 'friendly fire' on this day but as Norman L.R. Franks noted 'after days of air attack it was obviously a case of shoot first, question it later'[1].

The following day, 806 Squadron had a much better day when joining a number of Fighter Command squadrons flying patrols over the evacuation ships. The Luftwaffe's *Fliegerkorps* VIII had not been able to fly for several days due to

Five Rocs in formation, August 1940. Note the variation in camouflage and roundel patterns among the individual aircraft. The foremost aircraft appears to have had replacement cowling panels from other aircraft painted to the early wartime temperate sea scheme. Serials seem to have been obliterated for censorship purposes. (Central Press Photographs, courtesy of BAE Systems Brough Heritage)

---

* This is the closest incident I have found to the episode related in 'Strike from the Sky' as descriptions of the bloodied cockpit are similar in the case of Burton and the dead pilot of McKee's text. On the 31st May another Skua was damaged and crashed on landing though both aircrew survived. The legend of the Skua flown back to base with a dying pilot was evidently quite well known in air arm circles – Eric Brown refers to it in 'Wings of the Navy' as well. It is almost certainly mostly fiction - the anecdote of 28 Skuas and Rocs destroyed in one day cannot be taken seriously as no records attest to such a slaughter.

The same five Rocs in formation as on the previous page, August 1940. The flat underside of the Roc, lacking the bomb recess of the Skua, can be seen. (Central Press Photographs, courtesy of BAE Systems Brough Heritage)

low cloud cover, which rendered their Ju87 Stukas virtually useless. However, at lunchtime, the clouds cleared and the Luftwaffe was there in force. Two Skuas and a Roc attacked Ju88s which were bombing the ships off the coast. Sneaking up on the bombers as they were intent on their dives, the Roc was able to shoot down one of the '*Schnellbombers*' while a Skua claimed another damaged. This was to be the only 'destroyed' claim for the Roc in its career.

On 31st May nine Skuas of 801 Squadron took part in action alongside ten Albacores of 826 Squadron. Both squadrons dive-bombed targets around Nieuport; the Albacores went for the harbour with 250lb bombs, and later a road junction at Westende. 801 Squadron meanwhile looked for pontoon bridges in the area to attack to hold up the movement of German troops. They found none, and instead dive bombed a 'pier' (actually a partially cut bridge) on an island in a canal North-North-West of Nieuport, and scored several direct hits on this. A second sub-flight of three Skuas attacked two piers on the Nieuport foreshore and again scored direct hits.

On the way back to Detling, the Skuas were attacked by Messerschmitt Bf109s, and two of the dive bombers were shot down, though not without a fight and one of the Messerschmitts was claimed as a probable kill. Luckily the Messerschmitts broke off to attack Lockheed Hudsons of 206 Squadron which were patrolling that evening. Improbably, Norman Franks' 'The Air Battle over Dunkirk' claims the Hudsons waded into the fray to save the Skuas and in doing so shot down two Bf109s! In fact, the Hudsons confirmed the Skuas' claim.*

It has been suggested[2] that the bombing on the Nieuport foreshore prevented an attack by heavy German forces on the Dunkirk perimeter, which could have had dire consequences for the entire BEF. It is true that the 12th Infantry Division had beaten back a concerted attack earlier in the day and later reported that the buildup to a second attack had been disrupted as a result of bombing by British aircraft at around 5pm. The Skuas were in action in the later part of the day, and were in the region of the canal at Nieuport. The timings do not entirely match up – 801 Squadron's attack on the piers was not until around 8pm – but the value of the dive bombers in this crucial battle is apparent.

On 2nd June, numerous patrols were carried out from early in the morning over the columns of ships ferrying troops back from France, the Skuas joining Hudsons and Blenheims. The crews could see everything from merchant ships to fishing boats crammed with soldiers, and even a tug towing a lifeboat both of which were crammed with men. On the following day a greater contrast would be hard to imagine; there were hardly any German aircraft over the Channel and the squadron diary states there was 'nothing to report'. The three Skuas and three Rocs patrolled at 4,000ft around the North Foreland in weather that was clear as a bell with fifteen miles' visibility and no cloud, and saw nothing. The evacuation was all but over. However, the Battle of France continued to rage and Channel convoys were now more vulnerable than ever – the Skua's and Roc's work was to continue.

The next mission for 801 Squadron did not take place until the 9th June, with numerous convoy escorts taking place. Similar missions were undertaken on the 11th and 12th, though poor visibility made the convoys hard to locate. While part of the squadron searched in vain for convoys in the mist, the rest of the Skuas attacked 'E' Boats in Boulogne harbour. These fast torpedo boats, otherwise known as *Schnellboots*, were playing havoc with Channel convoys and would continue to do so into July.

At around 1235 hours the Skuas and Rocs dive bombed the harbour where the 'E' boats were moored and strafed the boats themselves. The Flight Commander suggested another attack with the addition of 20lb bombs in Light Series carriers and at 1525 the flight of five aircraft took off for the day's second operation. After the first attack the 'E' boats had been moved across the harbour, but were no less vulnerable. The five aircraft attacked, dropping three 250lb bombs and 40 20lb bombs. One 'E' boat suffered several direct hits and two others were damaged. A jetty was also hit and as the Skuas pulled up, they raked a row of parked lorries loaded with soldiers.

That night another Skua was operating above the evacuation. Pilot Officer Clarke's yellow and black striped target tug Skua was assigned to a novel task, towing a lighted flare above the sea north of the ferry channel to allow Coastal

---

* *This is unsurprising in a book that drastically underplays the efforts of the Fleet Air Arm during the evacuation. Franks also suggests the incident took place a day later on 1st June*

A section of Blackburn Rocs peels off into a dive bombing run. Whilst primarily intended as a fighter, the Roc could carry 660lb of bombs under the wings. Rocs were used by 801 Squadron to dive bomb targets in France during the Dunkirk evacuation. (Fleet Air Arm Museum)

Command Avro Ansons to bomb any 'E' boats that might try to attack the evacuation ships, along with a Fairey Battle, also of No. 2 Anti Aircraft Co-operation unit. The experience was, according to Clarke, 'as if we had flown inside an electric light bulb'. All the two aircraft could do was patrol up and down between Dunkirk and the River Scheldt, blinded by the light of their own flares, hoping there were no night fighters in the area.

'For three-quarters of an hour I sweated a blind course up the Belgian and Dutch coast,' said Clarke. 'I never saw a thing, neither land, sea nor Ansons. All I had for guidance were my instruments – how I wished that I had spent more hours under a hood – and some rough courses worked out by the Navigation Officer at Detling.'[3]

Clarke had several lucky escapes that night. An unidentified aircraft collided with the towing cable, severing it but not damaging the Skua, while on the way home he was fixed in the glare of searchlights at Dover and narrowly avoided crashing into the sea. On the positive side, the Coastal Command Ansons claimed one 'E' boat destroyed.

Over the next couple of days the Fleet Air Arm Skuas and Rocs undertook more convoy escort patrols and photo reconnaissance missions. One of these turned sour when Lieutenant Collett was sent to reconnoitre Boulogne and photograph a new battery being constructed near Calais. The Skua came under heavy anti-aircraft fire and the port wing was almost blown off. Collett limped back to Manston with shrapnel in his abdomen and his port fuel tank pierced and leaking – another testament to the strength of the Skua, but also to the vulnerability of the crew and the non self-sealing fuel tanks.

More convoy and reconnaissance missions followed, but on 20th June, 801 Squadron dive bombed heavy gun emplacements, possibly those that Lieutenant Collett was photographing when he was hit by AA fire. A large battery was being installed at Cap Blanc Nez and four Skuas and five Rocs of 801 were despatched to bomb the emplacement. This time it appeared the lessons of the past had been learned – the disastrous attack on the *Scharnhorst* had taken place only the previous week – and fighter escort was on hand. Twelve Hurricanes from Croydon met the Blackburns before they set out over the Channel. At 1440 the squadron attacked from the sea in line astern. From 2,000ft they dived to 1,000ft dropping their bombs. The defences were initially caught off guard but by the time the third sub-flight had winged-over into the dive, the AA batteries were blazing into the sky. Sub-Lieutenant Day and Naval Airman Berry's Roc was hit as it dived, and plunged into the sea in a wreath of black smoke. The others pressed home their attack and scored four direct hits and a number of near misses. The Commanding Officer praised the Hurricanes for their co-operation, on one of the few occasions when the dive bombers were fortunate enough to have proper fighter escort.

Shortly after this episode, 801 Squadron would be released from Coastal Command control and return to Hatston. Meanwhile 800 and 803 Squadrons had returned from Norway a few days prior to 801 Squadron's last mission over the Channel. At the end of June *Ark Royal*, taking 800 and 803 with her again, was bound for the Mediterranean.

---

1   Norman L.R. Franks, *The Air Battle of Dunkirk*, p.85
2   Peter C. Smith, *Skua!*, pp. 164-5. See also John Dell's excellent Skua website http://freespace.virgin.net/john.dell/blackburn_skua.htm
3   Squadron Leader D.H. Clarke, *RAF Flying Review*, December 1959

Return to Norway...

It was not the end of operations over the country. Almost as soon as the withdrawal was complete, the FAA planned to harass German forces in Norway and damage facilities that helped the German war effort. The Skua's ability as a long range strike aircraft was recognised and 801 Squadron, back from helping to cover the Dunkirk evacuation, was earmarked to continue attacks against German interests in Norway. In particular, fuel and oil installations were regarded as valuable targets likely to cause difficulty to the enemy and eminently suitable for dive bombing attacks – 801 would make a number of attacks on this type of target over the coming months. The Squadron was now exclusively a Skua unit and had divested itself of its Rocs – the turret fighters no longer had a role as a frontline aircraft. They were just too slow and ungainly to be effective against enemy aircraft, with numerous shortcomings in the operation of the turret from a small aircraft. The short range compared to the Skua divested the Roc of its elder sibling's main advantage as a patrol fighter and the Roc could not carry the 500lb SAP bomb.

Some improvements meanwhile had been made to the Skuas. Photographs of 801 Squadron's aircraft at this time show armoured glass had been added to the windscreen and metal panels added to cover some of the less useful glazing.

The Officer Commanding 801 Squadron when it returned to Hatson was Lieutenant I.R. Sarel. The squadron had returned to Hatston after its tumultuous stint operating from Detling and its first mission back over Norway was scheduled for 3rd July. Several targets were identified in the Bergen area, the main target being the oil tanks at Eidsvag. The secondary target was 200 'prepared boats' reported by reconnaissance at Laksevag.

The Skuas took off just after midday and made for Bergen, each armed with a 250lb General Purpose bomb and light series racks loaded with 20lb high explosive 'Cooper' bombs. The squadron ran into heavy cloud over the target which prevented a search of the target area, and neither the fuel tanks or the boats could be located, though the photographs taken by some of the observers revealed that there were more fuel tanks in the vicinity of Lillevag.

As neither target had been located, each of the five aircraft attacked separate 'targets of opportunity'. The lead aircraft bombed a moored seaplane and sheds, the second aircraft attacked a oil tanker and escort vessel, the third aircraft three unidentified round structures on Vagenes Point, the fourth aircraft a hangar and slipway on Sotra Island and the fifth aircraft an oil tanker at Lillevag. All the Skuas dive-bombed their targets, and some made more than one attack, releasing their 250lb bomb first then following the initial strike with 20lb bombs. As the attacks were made separately, there were few opportunities to observe the damage made by each others' attempts. The crew of the fourth aircraft saw the seaplane hangar they had bombed smoking, but this was the only sign of success the squadron was able to observe.

While this was not a conspicuously successful raid it was good experience for the crews and it paved the way for future attacks. The fuel tanks that had been noted at Lillevag were slated as the next target for the Skuas, and four days later eight aircraft took off from Hatston on a course for Sotra.

The previous raid had been largely unopposed but this time, despite the raid taking place in the early hours of the morning, the aircraft faced heavy fire from shore based AA batteries. While the Skuas tried to attack by sections in line astern as they had trained, the aircraft had difficulty keeping station under the hail of flak. Three aircraft had to break away during the approach, and turned their attack on hangars on Sotra Island instead, while one aircraft turned away during the approach and made a second attempt on the fuel tanks alone. The aircraft released their bombs at around 2,500ft which was higher than usual, probably due to the intense flak.

The Skuas that were able to press their attack home were successful, as by the time the aircraft turned for home the tanks were shrouded in thick black smoke, with fires seen burning. Lieutenant H.S. Hayes, the squadron's senior observer, was praised for his efforts in guiding the squadron to the target by dead reckoning above the thick cloud.

More fuel tanks, this time at Dolvik, were identified for the Skuas to hit next. The attack took place on the 26th July in poor weather conditions. This made navigation difficult and the nine 801 squadron Skuas found themselves off course so they decided to attack the best nearby target rather than try to find the tanks. Unfortunately, while turning in cloud two of the Skuas collided. One evidently crashed while the other limped back to Sumburgh in the Shetlands. The two crew members of the first aircraft were lost and the Observer of the surviving aircraft suffered a broken arm as a result of crash landing.

The seven remaining Skuas continued, and dive bombed a large motor vessel of between 3,000 and 4,000 tons. The Skuas scored a hit directly amidships, and two near misses by the stern. The ship slewed to port and stopped, and the crew abandoned ship. The vessel was seen to be on fire and sinking by the stern.

This attack had proved once again that Skuas could be accurate and effective against even moving vessels, providing they were not heavily armoured or defended by flak and fighters. Sadly, it had also proved the dangers of operating so far from base in poor visibility, as one aircraft and crew had been lost, and another aircraft heavily damaged and an observer injured.

On 1st August 801 undertook two sorties over Norway with the aim of locating and photographing suitable targets around Bomlaford and Fanafjord, and attacking the telegraph stations at Slatteroy and Marstein. The objective of the attacks on the telegraph stations was as much to disguise the reconnaissance as to do real damage, but the attack was carried out professionally and a number of hits were scored around the telegraph masts.

The second sortie of the day was made by three Skuas which successfully located the Shell Company fuel tanks at Dolvik which they had failed to locate on the previous mission. The tanks were well camouflaged from the air but the photographs revealed their presence. The aircraft also successfully bombed a merchant ship in Korsfjord, which the crew abandoned, and had a few Cooper bombs left for a strike on Marstein W/T station as well. A third mission had been planned but was cancelled due to poor weather.

With the important fuel tanks at Dolvik now located, the squadron lost little time in returning to attack the target. Nine Skuas led by Lieutenant E.G. Savage took off from Hatston in the early afternoon, though one developed engine

Skua L2890 of 801 Squadron in 1940. The aircraft was flown on occasion by Lieutenant (later Captain) R.W. Harrington who flew L2890 when attacking Bergen in July 1940. The aircraft was damaged by flak but brought its crew safely back to Hatston. Note the apparent lack of a code letter – colour schemes went through many changes in the middle of 1940. (Fleet Air Arm Museum)

trouble and had to return. The eight other Skuas pressed on and attacked the tanks at just after 4pm UK time.

The dive bombing attack was carried out again in sections, line astern. The Skuas bore down on the storage tanks at 60 degrees, releasing their 250lb bombs at 1,000ft – the ideal bomb run for the aircraft. The results were devastating. The first bomb landed squarely between the two tanks causing fuel to slop over the surrounding area, helping fires to take hold. After Petty Officer Kimber's bomb hit, the largest tank exploded spectacularly and was soon burning fiercely. The second tank was seen to be holed and burning and reconnaissance after the attack showed that the third was badly cracked and incapable of storing fuel. A single anti-aircraft gun had begun firing at the Skuas as they started their dive but it was silenced as soon as the first explosion took place and none of the aircraft were damaged. Lieutenant Hayes was mentioned in despatches for this mission and the DNAD remarked that it was a 'well executed attack'[1].

A pilot who was called to take part in occasional missions with 801 Squadron later found fame as one of the foremost test pilots of the wartime and postwar periods. Lieutenant, later Captain, Eric Brown (mystifyingly known to all as 'Winkle') flew with the squadron, to help cover attrition, when they attacked the fuel tanks in the vicinity of Bergen. His account provides a sobering view of the dangers of this kind of mission:

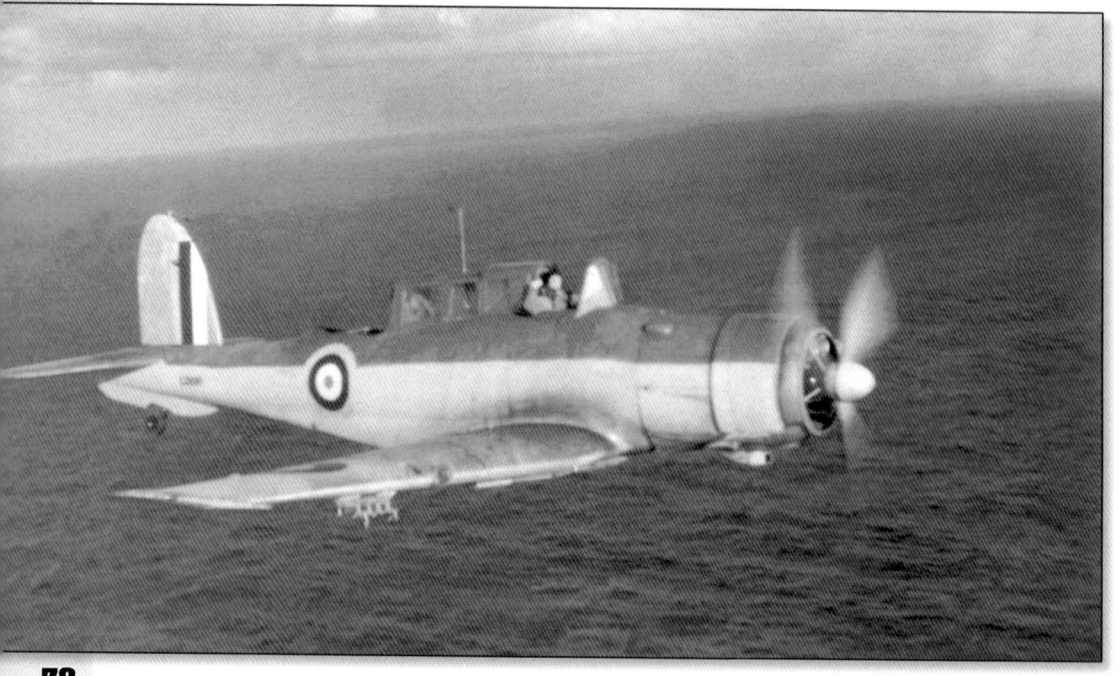

'We were flying out of Hatston – that was a tight trip for distance. We took off, we went to Bergen and climbed up. We hadn't met any opposition at that point, we were at about 10,000ft and we came in and dived down on the oil tanks. Not from 10,000ft – we came down a bit from ten because we wanted to have a bit of speed over the target, so we dived from about, I would say, six or seven thousand and dropped our bombs on the oil tanks. We seemed to get a few hits - then we collected a shoal of Me109s, and they pursued us along the fjord. I clung to the fjord wall and that meant they could only attack me from one side, and I was very close to the water so they couldn't attack me from below. The only way they could do it was from above and the left. And when we did have one come in on us, the way I got rid of him was to put out the dive brakes suddenly. He got the shock of his life because we slowed right up, he had to take violent evasive action and he left us pretty well alone after that. He fired on us, and he hit us before he broke away, but not very much.'[2]

The weather was also proving problematic with these dangerous and distant missions, as the Skua had precious little spare endurance for missions from Hatston to Norway. The station commander at Hatston expressed concern about continuing these attacks with relatively few aircraft, but was urged by the Vice Admiral of Orkney and Shetlands to continue them whenever possible. The missions continued through August and into September. The fuel storage tanks at Dolvik were hit again. In addition, shipping and telegraph stations were attacked with varying degrees of success. The squadron also embarked on HMS *Furious* for several missions which enabled them to take part in operations with Swordfish. On the 3rd September they attacked shipping and shore facilities, and again on the 7th when they sunk a supply ship and damaged a warehouse. From Hatston two days later the squadron surveyed the damage they had done to the fuel tanks at Dolvik (by now only one was standing and was severely cracked) and bombed a 2,000 ton motor vessel which was afterwards observed to be listing. The second section attacked another ship at Haugesund, and scored a hit on the ship ahead of the funnel as well as damaging the jetty.

The fuel tanks at Dolvik, near Bergen, after they were dive bombed successfully by Skuas of 801 Squadron (National Archives)

Later in the month 801 embarked on *Furious* for attacks on Tromso and coastal shipping. Several Skuas were lost during this phase of operations which called the whole nature of attacks against Norwegian targets into question. The Skuas regularly faced enemy aircraft and their endurance was so marginal that any fighting near the target drastically reduced their ability to return safely. The performance of the Skua against the Luftwaffe's fighters was also becoming a factor again. Two aircraft were lost on the mission of the 13th of September when eight Skuas attacked the oil installation at Skalevik and another on the 22nd when attacking shipping in Trondheim harbour. One Skua, that of Petty Officer E.G.R. Harwin and Naval Airman J.R. Maunder, was shot down by Feldwebel Harbach in a Messerschmitt Bf109. On the 22nd, Sub-Lieutenant B.F. Wigginton and K.R. King lost its way in fog and could not locate *Furious*, so set a course for neutral Sweden rather than face captivity.

The attacks continued into October. On the 2nd, eleven Skuas of 801 Squadron took part in two separate strikes on shipping, with one ship hit and set on fire by the first flight at Haugesund, while a second ship was dive bombed by three of the Skuas at Bjornefjord and seen to be sinking. However, the Skuas were 'bounced' by fighters and one, L2929, was shot down in flames. The other Skuas were chased and had to resort to desperate manoeuvring to avoid the fate of their compatriot. A few of the Skuas were damaged but managed to escape into cloud and return to Hatston. The German forces in Norway were clearly learning and it was considered that they must have developed a warning system. The DNAD recommended that the Skuas only be sent after targets that had been identified by reconnaissance and were thought worthy of the risk. The Vice Admiral commanding the forces in Orkney and Shetland protested 'I cannot believe that Their Lordships really consider that an attack of this sort carried out by the finest dive bombers in the world constitutes an unacceptable risk'[3], but the number of raids dropped after this. There were no raids at all in November and only one in December.

Commander Howe's glowing praise for 801 squadron was noted, and Lieutenant Martyn was recommended for a decoration as he had taken part in 26 missions over Norway, and the Vice Admiral commanding the forces in Orkney praised his 'continued ability and determination'. He was awarded the DSO on the 30th October. Skua crews had won numerous decorations and mentions in despatches and were among the most battle hardened and skilled of the war. The crews of 801 Squadron were reportedly in high morale at the time, although this would not remain the case. In fact, by the time Howe wrote this, the increasing losses of the squadron were taking their toll. A fruitless month of operations in January 1941, where weather conditions led to the cancellation of all the planned missions over Norway, did not help matters. In February, 801 Squadron was moved to St. Merryn in Cornwall. The Skua's relationship with Norway was over.

---

1   National Archives, ADM 1/11333
2   Captain E. Brown in conversation with the author 20th August 2006
3   Letter from Admiral Commanding, Orkneys and Shetlands to Secretary of the Admiralty, 25th November 1940, ADM 1/11333

The Mediterranean

Ark Royal did not stay at Scapa Flow for long – her services, and those of her squadrons, were needed elsewhere. On 17th June 1940, three days after anchoring after returning from Norway, and less than a week after the *Scharnhorst* raid, the carrier left for the Mediterranean. A week previously, Mussolini had declared war on Britain and naval power in the Mediterranean was about to become of critical importance. Months earlier, *Ark Royal* had been in the area for training. Now, it was deadly serious.

Both 800 and 803 Squadrons, replenished with new aircraft, went to the new theatre of operations where a modern aircraft carrier with its large complement of aircraft was sorely needed. The elderly HMS *Eagle* was the only carrier currently there and was too slow and vulnerable for this combat zone. Facing Italy's modern and experienced navy, the *Regia Navale*, was bad enough, but things were about to get worse.

Fortunately the task force, known as Force H, was commanded by an officer with very high regard for the potential of air power at sea. While the Navy had been slow to accept the importance of aircraft during the Norwegian campaign, Admiral Somerville took every opportunity to use *Ark Royal*'s aircraft to increase the striking (and defensive) power of Force H. Moreover, he took to the air frequently and when there was a seat free would go up in a Skua while the fighters made mock attacks on *Ark Royal*'s Swordfish.

On the day *Ark Royal* sailed, the Government of France was taken over by a group led by Marshal Pétain who favoured a settlement with Germany. Negotiations between Pétain and Hitler over terms of surrender had started before the carrier had left British waters. Now Force H had not only the Italian fleet but potentially the powerful and modern French fleet to worry about as

Skua L3049 'L' of 800 Squadron on Ark Royal at Gibraltar, running up on deck while an officer talks to the pilot and a matelot uses his weight to prevent the tail rising in the propeller wash. The ship appears to be berthed in the harbour and the 'Rock' looms over the ship. (Fleet Air Arm Museum)

Skua 6L of 800 Squadron taking off from Ark Royal at the end of August 1940. Ark Royal, with Force H, was accompanying reinforcements to the Mediterranean Fleet to the Eastern side of that sea. Among these ships was HMS Illustrious, seen in the background. The Skua is launching on a fighter patrol above the fleet. (Fleet Air Arm Museum)

well. As the task force continued towards Gibraltar the situation continued to deteriorate. The British Government was determined that the French warships should not fall into German hands, and if they remained under the control of a defeated France this remained a dangerous possibility.

Force H and the Mediterranean Fleet sailed to the French anchorages at Mers El Kebir and Alexandria on the North African coast. Despite determined and repeated negotiation the French fleet refused all terms and Force H, after all ultimata had expired, began to bombard the moored ships. The 'disarmament' of the French fleet was known as Operation Catapult, and the Skuas' first role was to patrol over the British ships in case any French aircraft decided to attack. The irony that the Skuas were about to go into action against the country that days beforehand their compatriots in 801 and 806 Squadrons had been fighting to defend no doubt did not go unnoticed. Neither did the importance of the task. 'We didn't really know much about the politics of it,' said 800 Squadron Armourer Ron Jordan, 'but we knew that if the French fleet decided to join with the Italians we'd have been overwhelmed. Malta would have been lost and then all the convoys would have had to have gone round the Cape'. Much was at stake.

Although there were numerous French fighters in the vicinity during the bombardment, none attacked the patrolling Skuas. However, as the bombardment came to a close, a twin-engined Martin approached the Skuas and shot one down before being set upon by the rest of the squadron and destroyed.

The British ships ceased firing just after six o'clock as the French ships were no longer returning fire. They were in some disarray, the *Dunkerque* had been beached and several other ships were on fire. However, shortly afterwards, the

An enlargement of the previous photo, shows a darker underside to Skua 6L, which also appears in stills from the film 'Ships with Wings'. The demarcation line, just above the exhaust, seems to show a different tone underside, which is possibly a blue such as azure or light Mediterranean blue. A member of Ark Royal personnel from this theatre recalled seeing some Skuas repainted in blue shortly after joining Force H. It is likely that the darker underside colour did not last long - later photographs show no sign of it.

battleship *Strasbourg* was seen making for open sea with two destroyers, and Ark's Swordfish were armed with 250lb GP and 500lb SAP bombs. A flight of Skuas was detailed to escort them. One bomb hit the ship, but two Swordfish were shot down. A further wave of Swordfish, this time armed with torpedoes, followed up the attack as HMS *Hood* gave chase, but the strike was unsuccessful; the sun had already set by the time the Swordfish were in place to launch their torpedoes.

The day ended with the loss of five aircraft, two of them Skuas – one of which was that shot down by the French aircraft, and another which had to ditch near the *Ark Royal*. Apart from that of the first Skua, all the crews were recovered. The operations had been somewhat unsatisfactory, partly because flying from *Ark* was disrupted by the bombardment and no offensive operations took place until after both sides had stopped firing.

Force H withdrew to Gibraltar for two days before returning to Mers el Kebir for Operation Lever – finishing off the *Dunkerque*. Three waves of Swordfish were escorted by six Skuas, with more success than those pursuing the *Strasbourg* had enjoyed. The first wave scored several hits, as did the second wave. One torpedo struck a tug which was loaded with mines, causing an enormous explosion. Initially the Swordfish and their escorting Skuas met little resistance, but as the third wave went in the Skuas were engaged by numerous French aircraft. According to the Admiralty report[1], the French fighters thoroughly outmanoeuvred the Skuas, though they apparently did not press their superiority. Perhaps the fighters preferred to try and disrupt the attack, but equally it may be supposed that attacking such recent allies did not come easily. Several of the Skuas were damaged by gunfire and all but one made it back to *Ark Royal*, though the shot down crew was rescued.

The day after Operation Lever the Mediterranean fleet sailed from Alexandria to protect two convoys leaving from Malta carrying civilian evacuees.

At the same time, HMS *Illustrious* and 806 Squadron were working up in preparation for joining the Mediterranean Fleet and adding a second modern carrier to *Ark Royal*. Things were not going entirely smoothly however. The squadron, which had supposedly re-equipped with Fulmars, still carried several

Skuas to make up numbers as the Fulmar had some teething problems in early squadron service. The fighter squadron had of course been formed months earlier and had seen a great deal of action, but had not operated from an aircraft carrier due to the Norwegian campaign and the evacuation from Dunkirk. Although 806 had taken on a number of the new Fairey fighters, six were written off within days of the squadron joining *Illustrious* in June 1940, mainly in landing accidents. It appears that the Squadron Commander, Lieutenant Charles Evans, a veteran of 803 Squadron from the beginning of the war, preferred to stick to his Skua and was still flying one into July. Although the Fulmars were better armed than the Skuas, and slightly faster, they were heavier, had no rear armament and were more difficult to maintain.

Before *Illustrious* joined the Mediterranean Fleet, she worked up in Bermuda where even the Skua's deck landing characteristics were tested to the limit. The fighters had not had much opportunity to train on the way out because of gale force winds. While anchored at Bermuda, two Fulmars and six Skuas took off to undergo much needed practice, but while they were up, the wind dropped away to nothing. With their fuel running low, and no airfield on the island to divert to, there was no option but to try and land on the stationary carrier. Two Skuas and both the Fulmars got down in one piece, but Evans' Skua hit the carrier's island, the next Skua went over the bow and another made it down but skidded on landing and came to rest with the tail hanging over the side. The final Skua tore its arrestor hook out and surged back into the air. With no way of safely getting back on deck, and precious little fuel left, the pilot Roger Nicholls was told by Captain Boyd to try his luck putting down on Bermuda's golf course. The resulting landing wiped both wings off while the engine broke free and,

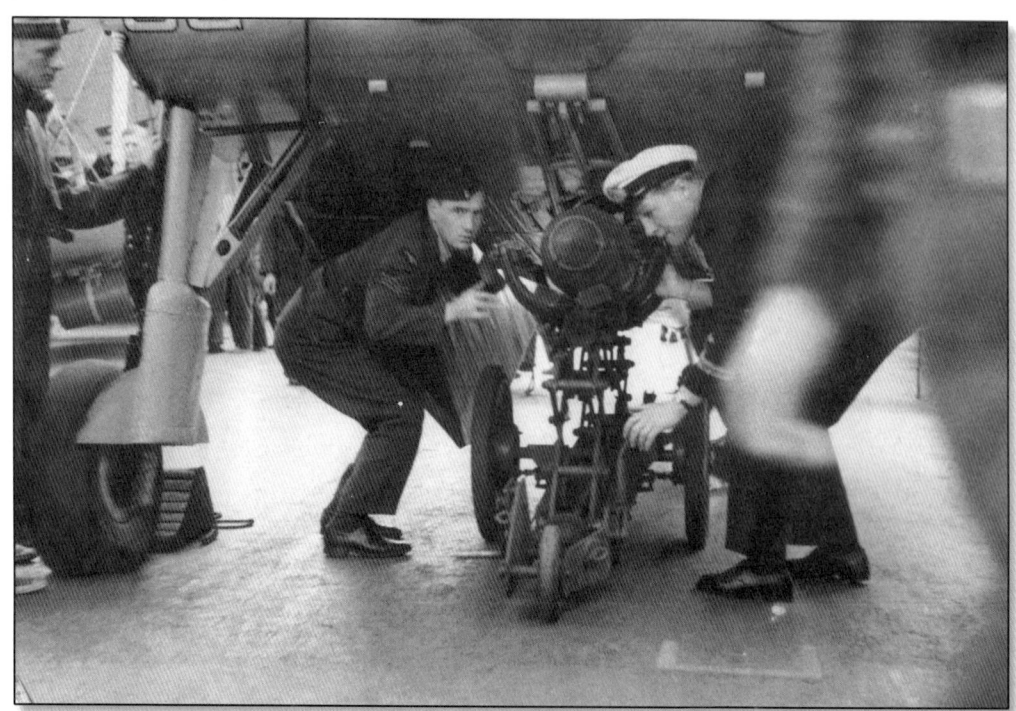

Skua 6G of 800 Squadron being bombed up in the Mediterranean. A naval officer and a RAF 'maintainer' move the device, possibly a 500lb SAP, into position. The bomb appears to be a live round, possibly for the attack on Italian cruisers at Cape Spartivento or the French battleship Richelieu. (Fleet Air Arm Museum)

according to one witness, scored a 'hole in one' on the 17th. The battered *Perseus* XII was subsequently presented to the Mid Ocean Golf Club[2].

On the 9th of July, the Skuas from *Ark Royal* had their first brush with the second 'new' enemy in the space of a week – this time the Italian Regia Aeronautica. A three-engined CANT Z506B seaplane appeared, shadowing Force H and a flight led by Lieutenant R.M. Smeeton launched to meet it. The first Italian air force victim of *Ark Royal* fell to the guns of 800 Squadron.

However, the shadower had reported the British position and Force H was attacked by 40 Savoia-Marchetti SM79 *Sparviero* (Hawk) bombers. The raiding aircraft were flying very high and the bombing was more accurate than the *Ark Royal*s had come to expect from the Luftwaffe in Norway. The battle-hardened crews of 800 and 803 Squadron acquitted themselves well against the fragile bombers, with four destroyed and two heavily damaged. At full speed the SM79 was as fast as a Skua but of mixed steel tube, wood and fabric construction and lacking the protection the Luftwaffe bombers had. Force H got away with nothing but near misses (Italy claimed *Hood* and *Ark Royal* had been put out of action) but the lesson had been an uncomfortable one. Midshipman (later Lieutenant Commander) 'Mike' Lithgow noted: 'the Regia Aeronautica made some determined efforts to sink the Ark, and on several occasions undertook

Skuas of 800 Squadron ranged on the deck of Ark Royal in the Mediterranean, in company with a number of Swordfish. Although the image purports to be from January 1941, it could in fact depict the range for one of the raids in early February, against the Tiso dam, Livorno, La Spezia and Genoa, over which Skuas maintained fighter patrols. (Fleet Air Arm Museum)

some beautiful high-level bombing runs in the face of heavy AA fire and attacks from our Fulmars and Skuas'[3]. The Skua pilots were often pleased to be in the air at the time as it was considered safer than being on the ship – such was the threat the bombing posed.

The need for a fighter control system like the one that worked so well in the Battle of Britain was apparent. One disadvantage *Ark Royal* had compared to *Illustrious* was her lack of radar – Ark had to rely on that of a 'picket ship' like *Curlew* or *Sheffield*, which made the control process harder as information had to be relayed to Ark before it could be used to direct the fighters.

At the beginning of August, the Skuas reprised the escort role they had played in Norway, with Operation Hurry. Vital Hurricanes for the defence of Malta flew from HMS *Argus*, a Skua leading each flight – as a two seat aircraft with navigator on board as well as ample endurance the Skua was an ideal guide. All twelve Hurricanes and the two Skua guides reached the island safely.

By the end of August *Illustrious* had joined *Eagle* with the main body of the Mediterranean Fleet. Some accounts say that 806 had now standardised on the Fulmar, and the newer fighter was used whenever possible. However, serviceability of the Fulmar was still poor and Skuas (and indeed some Sea Gladiators) were retained for when insufficient Fulmars were available.

The Regia Aeronautica started further attacks at the end of August. On the 31st, Lieutenant Spurway of 800 Squadron chased a shadowing CANT for 60 miles until he was finally able to overhaul and shoot down the seaplane. Fighter patrols were mounted, but the Mediterranean was unseasonably cloudy that day and the bombers didn't find their target. Meanwhile, *Ark Royal* was about to get a chance to even the score.

Skua '6M' of 800 Squadron in the Mediterranean, late 1940 or early 1941. When 800 Squadron joined Force H in the Mediterranean, where the squadron operated between July 1940 and April 1941, the colour scheme changed to Sky lower surfaces, code letters moved to the fuselage from the fin, and the code reproduced on the wing root. (Fleet Air Arm Museum)

Over the next couple of days the Skuas took part in the colourfully named Operations Smash and Grab. The fighters were to escort the attacking Swordfish to and from the target, Cagliari airfield. These raids were carried out under cover of darkness and were a great success. Force H expected reprisals but no Italian aircraft appeared. 'Grab' turned out to be a diversion for a convoy of army reinforcements to Libya, but was nonetheless a satisfying opportunity for the *Ark Royal* aircrews to take the fight to the enemy.

The Skua crews on *Ark Royal* left the Italians for a short time while Force H attended to unfinished business. A joint force of British and Free French troops aimed to take the French stronghold at Dakar from the forces loyal to Pétain's government. On 14th September a lone Skua photographed the defences at Dakar, and pilot Lieutenant Enever reported six warships in the roads and the harbour itself. The following day two more Skuas reconnoitred the port and identified the warships *Georges Leygues*, *Gloire* and *Montcalm* as well as the newly completed battleship *Richelieu* – a more modern and heavily armed ship than any the British could muster in the Mediterranean and a genuine threat to British naval supremacy in the region if France turned to open hostility.

At first, the task force tried to persuade any wavering French combatants in Dakar to rejoin the Allied cause. Swordfish from *Ark Royal*'s squadrons, together with some small French training biplanes, dropped leaflets exhorting the troops to down arms and leave their posts. Optimistically, the British and Free French leaders thought that faced with the possibility of attack by their countrymen, the forces holding Dakar would join the Free French cause. Unfortunately, it seemed Allied intelligence had misjudged the prevailing attitude in Dakar (which

"Goodbye 800 Sq". An emotional moment as 800 Squadron prepares to leave Ark Royal in April 1941 – this marks the final range of Skuas on an operational aircraft carrier. They are about to transfer to HMS Furious, which has brought the Fulmars of 807 Squadron as replacements. (Fleet Air Arm Museum)

had soured against the Allies considerably since Mers El Kebir) as well as the strength of defence. The town was not about to give up.

Skuas from *Ark Royal* provided air cover for the attack on 23rd September, which met fierce resistance and resulted in heavy casualties. The following day Force H determined to attack the French warships and the Skuas of 800 and 803 undertook their first dive bombing attack since the *Scharnhorst* raid in June.

Early that morning, six Skuas of 800 Squadron took off out of the mist and headed towards the *Richelieu*. Defences were light – there were no opposing fighters and only a few anti-aircraft guns were firing from the battleship, which may have been affected by the poor visibility. As the Skuas formed line-astern and peeled off to attack they were faced with the same problem, a layer of haze hanging over the ship – nothing better than a near miss was achieved. Neither Skua squadron had been ashore for long enough to do much dive-bomber training in months, and many of the experienced crews had been killed or captured in the attack on the *Scharnhorst*. All of these factors possibly contributed to the lack of a single hit, but at least on this occasion all the aircraft returned safely. It is difficult to imagine anyway how six Skuas could have done worthwhile damage to such a heavily armoured vessel.

More Skuas escorted *Ark Royal*'s Swordfish on a strike against the cruisers *Georges Leygues* and *Montcalm* but they had no more luck than 800 Squadron. The following day Operation Menace was called off, and shortly afterwards, *Ark Royal* sailed for the UK. A squadron with Fulmars, number 808, joined the Skuas of 800 Squadron, who remained with the ship they had been with

A rather worn and weathered target towing Roc, possibly L3154, operated by 775 Sqdn, at Dekheila. It is painted in the original FAA Temperate Sea Scheme, with night/ white wing undersides. In the background is an RAF Douglas Dakota. (Fleet Air Arm Museum)

for most of the war. It was the end of 803 Squadron's time on the Skua. They reformed shortly afterwards on the Fulmar.

In early November, *Ark Royal* was back with Force H in the Mediterranean. For the most part, the task force would be engaged in escorting fast convoys for Malta as well as bringing more fighters to the embattled island.

On the 8th, a shadowing CANT appeared and 800 Squadron Skuas shot it down. The Fulmars of 808 Squadron had their first chance to test their mettle during the ensuing bombing raid, and thanks to their efforts none of the bombers penetrated as far as the ships.

On 9th November, Swordfish from *Illustrious* attacked the Italian Fleet at Taranto, causing such damage that the balance of naval power in the region was altered more or less permanently. The Italians still had enough surface units to cause the Malta convoys a headache, but were no longer in a position to threaten merely as a 'fleet in being'. Effectively the attack forced the remainder of the Italian fleet out of port – ironically this would cause some short term problems for Force H. On the 17th, a second attempt to fly Hurricanes to Malta off *Argus* was staged, but due to the movements of Italian warships, the fighters and their Skua escorts had to launch from further west than had been planned. This time things did not go well and only four of the 12 Hurricanes reached Malta while the rest ran out of fuel and had to ditch.

Force H, in the western Mediterranean, often sailed out the straits of Gibraltar to provide some protection to Atlantic convoys from Sierra Leone and Capetown. This involved anti-submarine patrols by both the Swordfish and the Skuas – at times, the entire complement of *Ark Royal*'s aircraft were airborne at once. On 27th November, it became apparent that the usual routine of protect-

A company of officers watches the last of 800 Squadron's Skuas leave Ark Royal. Skuas had been based on Ark Royal from the end of 1938 but were replaced by Fulmars because Admiral Somerville felt the Skua's dive bombing abilities would not be necessary in the Western Mediterranean. (Fleet Air Arm Museum)

ing convoys was developing into something different. A force of Italian cruisers and battleships approaching from the north threatened the convoy, codenamed 'Corner'. Force H moved to engage, and what then developed was (later) called the Battle of Cape Spartivento. Swordfish from *Ark Royal* launched and made for the light grey Italian warships which were making full speed to the north. Several hits were made on the battleship *Vittorio Veneto* and a ship that was identified at the time as a cruiser but later turned out to be a destroyer. The latter was thought to have been disabled and seven Skuas led by Lieutenant Smeeton raced to the scene to finish her off. However, a Swordfish which was on anti-submarine patrol at the time reported that the 'disabled' ship had stopped but soon afterwards made off at high speed, which may explain why the Skuas were unable to locate her. Instead, they found a second cruiser squadron off Cape Teleuda and dive-bombed that. The results of this are unclear – the squadron claimed that two cruisers had been hit and that one had reduced speed as a result. The Italians claimed that one cruiser, the *Bolzano*, had been hit but later amended this to five near misses only. The flight found and shot down a reconnaissance Imam Romeo Ro.43 on the way back by way of consolation.

The Mediterranean Fleet was proving more of a handful to the Regia Aeronautica than was acceptable. The Taranto operation and the success of the Malta convoys had shaken the Axis powers, with the result that a specialised Luftwaffe anti-shipping force transferred to Sicily on the 10th December to bolster the Italians. This was none other than Fliegerkorps X – the Skuas' adversary in Norway. On the 10th January, sustained attacks by hundreds of Stukas and Heinkels put *Illustrious* out of action for a year. They tried again as she was docked in Malta for emergency repairs but the heavy armour protection and the *Illustrious* and port's anti-aircraft defences saved the ship. This was essentially a reprisal for Taranto - *Illustrious* lived to fight another day, but *Ark Royal* was once again the only modern aircraft carrier in the Mediterranean.

Rather than the horrific bombardment *Illustrious* faced, all Force H had to contend with at this time was ten SM79 bombers and an escort of Fiat CR42 fighters, which dazzled the Skuas with an aerobatic display seemingly more suited to pre-war airshows. The Fulmars of 808 went for the bombers while 800 Squadron's Skuas grappled with the fighter

A Skua from 800 or 803 Squadron following a collision with the crash barrier on Ark Royal in the Mediterranean. The crash barrier was introduced on this ship in the Mediterranean theatre, meaning landing-on could be achieved more quickly. The complex underside shape of the Skua is very much in evidence, as are the fully extended flaps. (Fleet Air Arm Museum)

escort. The CR42, although obsolescent as an interceptor, was still capable of outmanoeuvring the heavier Skua. Nevertheless, 800 Squadron suffered no damage and kept the fighters off 808 Squadron's back, although they were unable to do more than claim some of the Fiats as damaged.

The third operation to fly Hurricanes to Malta, Operation Winch, was set for 3rd April, taking into account the lessons of the previous attempts. Instead of flying from *Argus*, this time the Hurricanes would transfer to *Ark Royal* and fly directly from the newer carrier. Ark's longer flight deck enabled the Hurricanes a longer take-off run and, consequently, to carry more fuel. Once again the Skuas escorted the fighters to the island with no losses.

Three days later, *Ark Royal* returned to Gibraltar. HMS *Furious* had sailed from the UK with the Fulmars of 807 Squadron, and this squadron was due to replace 800 Squadron on *Ark Royal*. The Skuas ranged at the stern and, one by one, made the take-off run off the carrier for the final time. The Skua was no longer viable as a fleet fighter. The sustained aerial attacks on Allied shipping in the Mediterranean meant pure fighters were needed. Though the Skua remained a potent weapon as a dive bomber there was no room for dive bombers alongside the Swordfish. Rear Admiral Jameson summed up the feelings of the '*Ark Royals*' after the squadron had left: 'It was sad to see the old Skuas go. They might be outdated, slow and ridiculously lightly armed, but they had done splendid work and had saved the Ark on many occasions'[4].

This is L2957, the first of 800 squadron's aircraft to ready itself to transfer to HMS Furious for the journey back to Britain. This Skua has had armoured glass added to the windshield and metal panels cover the lower side panels for added protection. (Fleet Air Arm Museum)

---

1   Documents at the National Archives under ADM 234/317
2   David Wragg, Swordfish: the story of the Taranto raid, p.40
3   Lt. Commander 'Mike' Lithgow, Mach One, p.29
4   William Jameson, Ark Royal, p.120

The end

On the 19th of February 1941, 801 Squadron moved from Hatston to St. Merryn in Cornwall. From there they made one dive bombing raid. In March the Squadron was sent to attack a ship in the harbour at Alderney in the Channel Islands, and both the ship and a warehouse were hit. No-one knew it at the time, but this was probably the last dive bombing attack by Skuas.

The squadron was now well practiced at dive bombing, as it had been primarily used in the strike role since the previous summer. The badly publicised harassing campaign against Norwegian targets following the Allied withdrawal is perhaps the best indication of the Skua's prowess as a dive bomber. Despite all that had been learned about which targets were suitable and which were not, it seemed that those at the top were prepared to repeat a previous mistake.

The squadron was moved to the RAF station at St. Eval under Coastal Command when German warships started to appear at Brest. Early in April, aerial reconnaissance by the RAF revealed the battlecruisers *Scharnhorst* and *Gneisenau* had put into the French port. Various plans were considered and once again the idea of using Skuas to dive bomb capital ships came to the fore. One of the ships was in dock with the gates closed and a small vessel tied up across the entrance. The other was moored and protected by anti-torpedo booms. Bomber Command had failed to make an impression on the ships, and a torpedo attack was unlikely to be successful because of the booms and the vessel moored across the dock mouth.

The RAF reconnaissance photograph that showed the Scharnhorst and Gneisenau berthed at Brest, at the centre of the image. One ship is in a dock with a vessel moored across the entrance, and the other is tied up, surrounded by torpedo nets. The RN saw dive bombing as the only option. (National Archives)

The only alternative seemed to be dive bombing. The Director of Plans noted on 1st April: 'the result of a D/B hit would not be so effective as a T/B hit but would be likely to damage the ships severely. Under existing conditions a larger target is offered to D/B than to T/B attack and both ships could be attacked'[1]. The plan concluded that dive bombing attack by 801 and 816 Squadrons (the latter with Swordfish) on or around the 8th April could do some damage to the ships and more importantly, drive them to sea where British submarines were gathered. It was suggested that the attack be carried out at night under a full moon, as fighter escort was not available. The DNAD counselled caution, pointing out that the thickest armour a Skua could hope to penetrate with a 500lb SAP bomb was 2" and the two battlecruisers had armour more than twice as thick, so the attack might be costly and not achieve much.

Brest was one of the most heavily defended sites against aircraft attack in Western Europe at the time. The RAF frequently suffered heavy losses from flak and fighters even bombing at around 12,000ft. The Skuas would be required to dive to around 2,000ft in the interests of accuracy and doing the greatest possible damage. A further problem was the 'innumerable' searchlights, the intense glare of which at dive release altitude would virtually blind the pilots.

The Vice Chief of Naval Staff however thought that Skuas were 'the only aircraft that have a reasonable chance of hitting'[2]. He indicated that Skuas should be tried as the risks would not be greater than those faced by Ju87 squadrons – though bearing in mind the crippling losses suffered by Stukas during the Battle of Britain this is not as favourable as first it sounds. He pointed out 801's successful record in Norway and suggested that if the problem were simply one of efficiency, the squadron should be trained until it was sufficiently skilled.

In the end, the Naval Staff concluded that the planned attack would be too risky, and 801 Squadron was spared the fate of 800 and 803. In the light of the earlier attack on the *Scharnhorst* it is perhaps surprising that it was ever considered, but the fact remained that dive bombing was seen as the best way to accurately bomb a heavily defended target as small as a single ship. Without

A Skua squadron about to be bombed up. Though designed as a naval aircraft, the Skua saw much of its service operating from land bases. It was from such a base, RAF St. Eval, that Skuas made their last dive bombing mission, with 801 Squadron. (Fleet Air Arm Museum)

the Skua the Navy was going to be divested of that ability other than that which could be carried out by Swordfish and Albacores.

As a result of the plans for the Brest attack, 801 Squadron was closely examined. It was found to be wanting in morale and undertrained in areas such as night and formation flying, though its record and the skill of its pilots drew praise. It also appeared that the attrition the squadron had suffered, its turnover of personnel and the strain it had been subjected to had reduced the squadron's ability to dive bomb with the necessary precision, and practice on the nearby range at Padstow was disappointing. The Naval Staff therefore recommended that the aircrew be dispersed and the squadron reformed. In May 1941, the last frontline Skua squadron disbanded. It reformed on Sea Hurricanes in August and later in the war took part in Operation Tungsten, the Royal Navy's most successful dive bombing attack of the war where for the first time British naval dive bombers disabled a powerful capital ship, the *Tirpitz*. By this stage it appeared the painful lessons of the *Scharnhorst* had been learned – 42 Fairey Barracudas took part, protected by 80 fighters in a well-co-ordinated strike with the element of surprise – perhaps ironically, 801 was part of the fighter escort, flying Seafires.

It was to be the end of the squadron for the time being, but the end of the Skua in front line service for good. The Navy had incorporated dive bombing into the capabilities of the aircraft that was intended to fulfil the fighter role, and when a higher performance fighter was needed there was no longer any room for the Skua, however capable a dive bomber.

---

1   *Plan sent to DNAD 'Attack on Brest' 1st April 1941 from ADM1/11333*
2   *Response to 'Attack on Brest' 4th April 1941 by VCNS ADM1/11333*

Second line duties

The Skua was always intended to be adaptable to second line duties such as training and target towing. The production specification No.25/36 issued on 24th October 1936 requested that provision be made for 'target towing gear installation, which will be arranged as a conversion set'[1]. This would enable the Skua to deploy up to three sleeve or flag targets to train anti aircraft gunners, air gunners and fighter pilots.

Target towing tests had been carried out at the A&AEE with the first production Skua L2867, which Specification 25/36 had requested should be delivered with the relevant conversion set. Drogue towing trials were carried out during August 1939 with the Skua. The target towing gear consisted of a windmill driven cable drum, with 6,000ft of cable, attached to the starboard side of the fuselage adjacent to the rear cockpit. L3006 stayed at Brough for manufacturers' trials of the target towing gear.

Rocs could also be adapted for target towing, albeit with a greater degree of modification, and a number saw service in this configuration with specialist target towing units as well as training a frontline squadrons. The Roc's target towing ability was tested between March and September 1942 on one of the floatplane modifications, L3174. The turret was removed, and to the fuselage was fitted the B Mk IIA wind driven winch. The Roc target tug could deploy two 3ft diameter sleeve targets or three 5'5" flag targets.

The first Skua from the final batch, L3007, was painted in 3ft diagonal black stripes at 6ft intervals on a bright yellow background to show up against any background, the scheme subsequently adopted for all target towing aircraft. After the outbreak of war, the upper surfaces were painted in RAF or FAA camouflage but the undersurfaces retained their 'wasp' stripes.

A classic shot of Skua L3007 in flight. This machine was used to trial the black and yellow bands to identify target tug aircraft. Some accounts suggest it was also painted in red and white stripes during ditching trials, though no photographs exist of this scheme if it was ever worn. L3007 was later issued to 803 Squadron and served in the Mediterranean. (Fleet Air Arm Museum)

A gaggle of second-line Skuas at HMS Sparrowhawk (Hatston) in April 1942. Note the variety of colour schemes – the third aircraft in line (coded 'F') has the underside target-tug stripes, while 'R' and 'Q' (L2817) wear modified versions of the early-war temperate sea scheme. The furthermost aircraft 'T' has the later temperate sea scheme but appears to have the cowling from an earlier aircraft. (Fleet Air Arm Museum)

One of the largest users of Skuas and Rocs in the target towing role was No.2 Anti Aircraft Co-operation Unit based at RAF Gosport, which was hastily pressed into brief frontline service over the Dunkirk evacuation (see previous chapter). The unit had a number of Skuas from the beginning of the war and these were supplemented by 16 Rocs when the latter were phased out of frontline service. Unfortunately several of these were damaged when Stukas dive bombed the airfield during the Battle of Britain, and four Rocs were consequently stationed around the airfield as machine gun posts. Rocs were phased out as target tugs when Boulton-Paul Defiants became available.

The RAF was in fact an extensive user of the Skua and Roc and was initially assigned a larger share of Skuas than the Fleet Air Arm (102 against 88) but the RAF agreed to bolster the FAA's reserves by transferring its own Skuas.

Skuas and Rocs actually served on far more second line Naval squadrons than front line units. Skuas and Rocs were operated by 725, 755, 757, 758, 759, 760, 765, 767, 769, 770, 771, 772, 773, 774, 775, 776, 777, 778, 779, 780, 782, 787, 788, 789, 791, 792, 793, 794, and 797 Squadrons. The chief uses for Skuas and Rocs in these squadrons was as an advanced trainer and 'fleet requirements' – usually target towing to provide target practice for anti aircraft gunners.

The toughness of the airframe plus the extreme reliability of the Perseus engine (once teething problems had been resolved) as well as generally good handling made the Skua suitable for these roles. However, as in frontline service the performance left something to be desired. 'We fledgling naval fighter pilots who had been expecting to get into the 'hot rod' league forthwith could not help but wonder whether we had been sent to the right stable' opined Captain Eric Brown[2].

An incident with a 776 Squadron Skua in June 1942 provided more evidence of the extreme strength of the airframe. During the flight test of a Skua from Speke, the pilot had put the aircraft through its paces with a high-dive followed by some low-level flying when he happened upon a row of electricity pylons. There was no time to react and the Skua collided with the power cables. Leading Air Mechanic Mervyn Spencer Doe, the reluctant back seat passenger, stated: 'I learnt later from the electricity board that we had broken five out of eight cables'[3]. The Skua not only survived the incident, but was able to fly back to Speke.

Skuas and Rocs also served sporadically in the Air Sea Rescue role and it was a Roc, piloted by Pilot Officer D.H. Clarke, which took part in what is thought to be the only battle between two ASR aircraft – he claimed a Heinkel He59 damaged (see page 109).

Both Skua and Roc served in their less glamorous roles while the stock of parts allowed, and almost saw out the war. The last Skua in service, L3034, was struck off charge from 776 Squadron in March 1945.

---

1   Air Ministry Specification 25/36
2   Captain Eric Brown, Wings of the Navy, p.29
3   Flypast, June 2006, p.95

A Skua in the striped target-tug livery makes a low fly-by over RNAS Worthy Down. (Fleet Air Arm Museum)

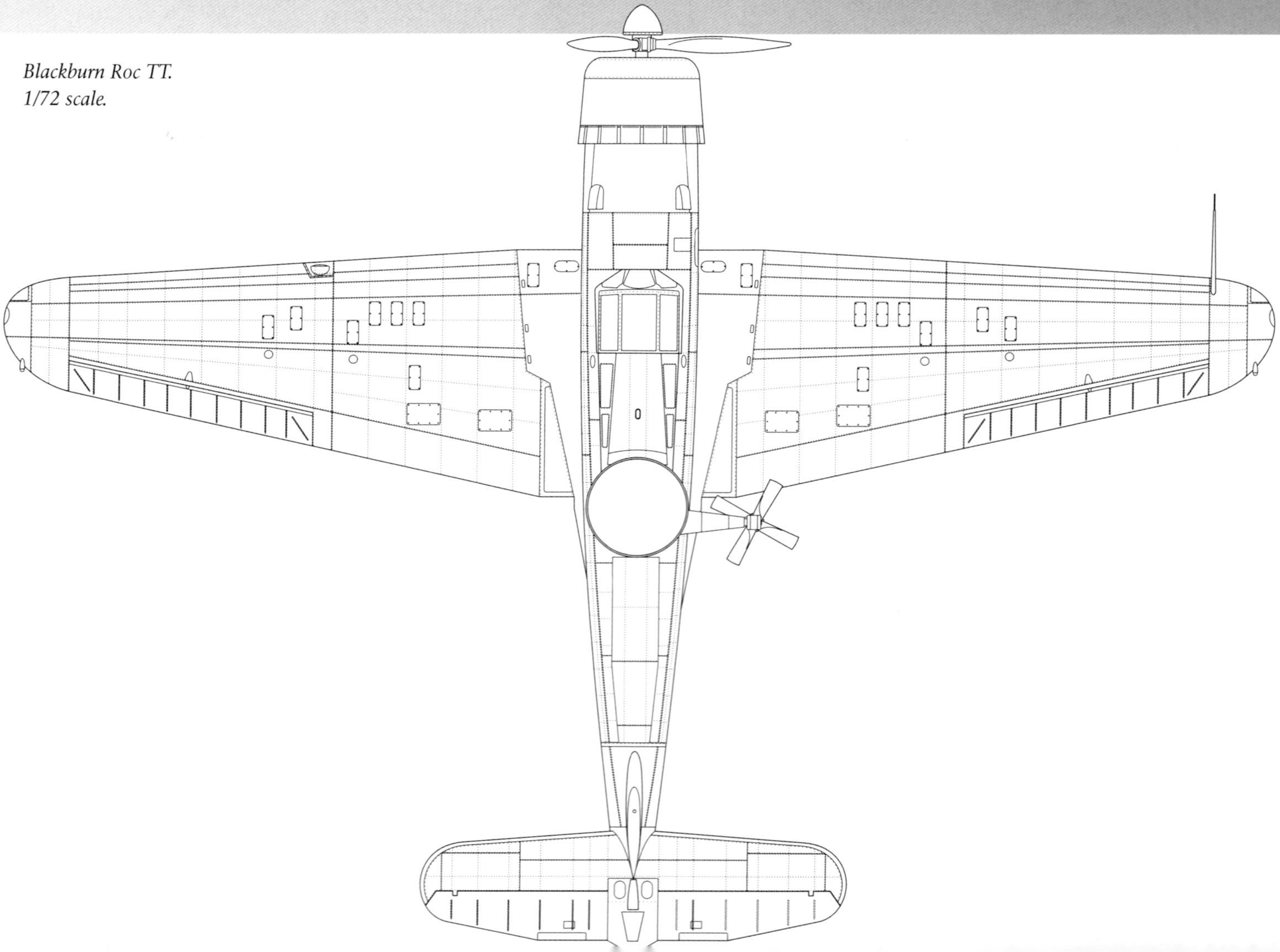

Blackburn Roc TT.
1/72 scale.

Blackburn Roc TT.
1/72 scale.

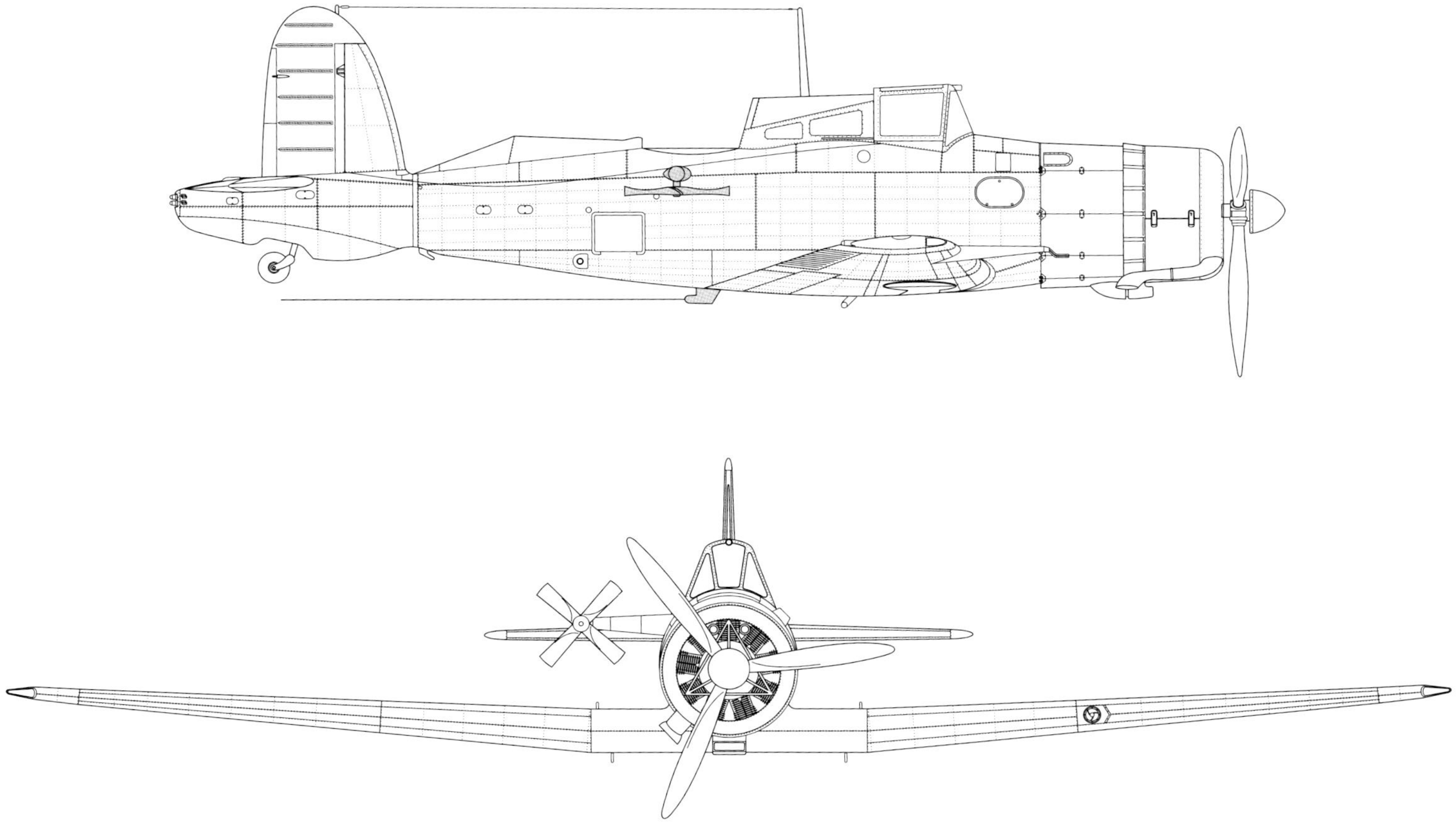

Blackburn Skua & Roc

99

Above: A target-towing Roc from RNAS Crail, possibly from 770 Squadron, in flight in 1942. The camouflage is probably a disruptive scheme of Extra Dark Sea Grey and Dark Slate Grey over Sky undersurfaces. *(Fleet Air Arm Museum)*
Below: A Roc, coded 'J' operating in the target-towing role flies above Orkney in 1941. *(Fleet Air Arm Museum)*

Above: A Roc 'J' from 771 (Fleet Requirements) Squadron in flight, operating from Hatston on Orkney in 1941. The aircraft has been modified for target towing with the removal of the turret, but retains its operational naval camouflage. (Fleet Air Arm Museum)

A target-towing Roc from 771 NAS comes to grief at RNAS Twatt on Orkney in 1942. Nose-overs on landing were not uncommon to Skuas and Rocs due to the long nose moment. This aircraft has had its turret removed and a wind-driven winch fitted. Fleet Air Arm Museum)

Maintainers from 771 (Fleet Requirements) Squadron attempt to right Roc L3187 after a landing accident at RNAS Twatt, Orkney on the 28th October 1942. The Roc carries bomb racks and still has its turret, suggesting it was used for training purposes rather than target towing. Camouflage has been modified from the original factory finish by deepening the upper demarcation and adding C-type roundels and fin flashes, though there are still no underwing roundels. (Fleet Air Arm Museum)

Future developments

There was no Blackburn Skua MkIII or Roc MkII. Relatively early in the career of the two aircraft the Air Ministry had decided that there was no more life in them. In March 1939 the Air Ministry confirmed that no Skuas beyond the 190 ordered would be required. Earlier still, in January 1938 the Admiralty ordered 127 Fairey Fulmars as insurance against the Roc failing completely.

There is evidence, albeit scanty, that Blackburn proposed a dedicated dive bomber version of the Skua for the RAF. Eric Brown recounts: 'Years later, the designer was to record Blackburn's regret at not being allowed to proceed with a simplified version of the Skua with a fixed undercarriage for the RAF as an answer to the "Stuka"' (at the 5th Sir George Cayley Memorial Lecture given by G.E. Petty in 1958)[1]. No further details of this aircraft are known – it does not appear to have reached the stage of a formal design study. However, the idea of a simple, strong fixed undercarriage appears to have inspired similar developments in other Skua and Roc related projects.

The design team at Blackburn no doubt felt that there was more development potential to come and when Specifications N.8/39 and N.9/39 as direct replacements for the Skua/Fulmar and Roc were issued, Blackburn submitted a design which owed much to the Skua. The two designs were structurally identical to the Skua but incorporated some surprising innovations, and lessons learned from the Skua. Blackburn specified a 1,500 horsepower Bristol Hercules for the N.8/39 and N.9/39, countering the Skua's greatest weakness – lack of power.

Of most surprise to the RAE was the 'low-drag fixed undercarriage,' which they felt was of 'special interest'. The Dowty-lever type legs (themselves quite unproven at the time) were shrouded by aerodynamic covers and could be jettisoned. Blackburn evidently wished to dispense with the reliability problems associated with retractable undercarriage and felt that the much simpler fixed units would help to keep serviceability high on long cruises in hostile conditions.

A further departure from Blackburn convention was the twin tail. This was partly to get around the maximum folded width of 13'6" which caused difficulties for all the manufacturers, being 2' narrower than the Skua which was already very compact when folded. Hawker, Gloster and Fairey tried various ways of folding the tail planes, while Supermarine tried to get away with a very small conventional tail within the width specified. Blackburn sought to get around the problem with a narrow, low aspect ratio tail plane with twin fins and rudders on the ends which increased the efficiency of the tail plane and elevators.

Visibility was better than average in the Skua, but Blackburn sought to improve this further. The Blackburn N.8/39 gave particular attention to visibility for the observer (which the RAE noted was at the expense of performance) by pinching in the fuselage around the rear cockpit. A further area of emphasis was

Blackburn's heavily delayed follow-up to the Skua was the Firebrand which began as a Hercules-engined two-seater closely developed from the Skua. It first saw the light of day after numerous changes including the powerplant becoming a Napier Sabre and the role to a single-seat interceptor. Skua lineage can be seen in the forward-set fin and square section fuselage at the wing root. (Author's collection)

landing speed. The RAE noted that Blackburn had employed their own slotted flap 'on which a considerable amount of wind tunnel work has already been done'. This was a development of the Skua flap which incorporated a much larger area of the lower surface of the wing and extended to the trailing edge, forming a slot as it deployed. The Skua's wing fold mechanism was proven to be strong, simple to operate and economical with hangar space, and was retained.

Blackburn had given a great deal of thought to the Skua's spin recovery problems and worked hard to eliminate these on the N.8/39. The wing tips were highly cambered and the twin tails would not be blanketed by the stabiliser or fuselage when in a spin. The RAE was so impressed by the likely spin characteristics of the N.8/39 that they felt model tests unnecessary.

Ultimately the RAE felt that the Blackburn's designs over-emphasised practicality and they preferred the aerodynamically uncompromising Supermarine despite concerns about its handling and safety. The Admiralty and Air Ministry were unhappy with all the responses, and were beginning to turn their mind to higher performance single seat fighters. They revised the specification and asked for higher performance single and two seat versions of N.8/39 while the turret fighter N.9/39 remained.

Blackburn went back to the drawing board and came up with a cleaner design with retractable undercarriage and a tail with similar layout to the Skua, a single fin well ahead of the tail plane. However, the wing flap arrangement was now even more radical, with full span slotted flaps and spoiler type ailerons which slid out of the wing's upper surface. The RAE was again very interested in this layout suggesting that it could potentially result in smaller, more efficient wings for high speed in flight but which could still give low landing speed and high controllability necessary for carrier landings. The Air Ministry was sufficiently impressed to order a small number of the Blackburn design to assess the wing layout, albeit in a less extreme form – partial span flaps and conventional ailerons. At this stage the design still had the Hercules engine. Although a single-seater the design had evolved from a two-seater and as a consequence was larger than the ideal.

This design evolved into the Firebrand, which had a development period that made the Skua's entry into service look smooth and rapid. The powerplant changed to the Napier Sabre, then the Bristol Centaurus, and much blood, sweat and tears went into ironing out the aircraft's numerous control problems. By the time the aircraft appeared, just like the Skua, it was ironically considered too heavy, too slow and too late.

---

1   Captain Eric Brown, *Wings of the Navy*, p.30

The Skua and Roc Described

Blackburn's design was the most modern of the submissions to Specification O.27/34. The fuselage was a metal stressed-skin construction in which the external plating was flush-riveted to longitudinal stringers over transverse frames. The fuselage was built in two pieces; the main fuselage ran from the firewall at the nose to a point just ahead of the tail fin, while the detachable rear fuselage incorporated the tail fin and stabiliser mountings and a strake under the fuselage, which improved directional stability and to which the tailwheel was mounted. The fuselage incorporated a hollow in the upper surface containing a liferaft, and the cover was fair with the top of the rear body. Unfortunately this worked better in theory than in practice and more often than not the emergency ring to release the dinghy would come off in the airmens' hands. The fuselage was circular in section along most of its length, apart from under and immediately aft of the wings where square fillets joined the mainplanes to the front body, giving the aircraft an 'Omega' [Ω] like section. Two watertight compartments, one under the front cockpit and another aft of the rear cockpit, were built in.

The cockpit was watertight up to the coaming and was enclosed by a long, framed glazing with a steep windscreen for good visibility in bad weather. The glass was totally un-armoured initially, although some attempts to improve protection were made after the Norwegian campaign. Armoured glass was added to the front panel of the windshield and metal panels were installed across the lower part of the outer windshield panels. The standard RAF blind flying panel formed the centre of the instrument panel. A MkII reflector gunsight was installed atop the instrument panel, and took up most of the front windscreen panel. A signal pistol was fitted in the floor with which different colour flares could be fired.

Two fuel tanks were installed in the middle of the cockpit on either side and these were not self-sealing.

The rear cockpit included a Fairey-type pillar for the rear gun which was housed in a recess in the rear fuselage when not in use. A quadrant-shaped glazing enclosing the rear cockpit could be swivelled back into the canopy when the rear gun needed to be used.

The rear cockpit was even more sparse than the front. Rather than a seat the Observer or TAG had only a thinly rubber-padded bench above the inner face of the bomb recess. To keep the TAG in place during diving and other violent manoeuvres, a 'G-string' was bolted to the floor to which the TAG or Observer could attach his harness. A bar could also be attached across the rear cockpit to give added support. 'It was horribly basic,' said Lloyd Richards, TAG with 803 Squadron. 'There was a vaguely padded pad to sit on. It was very stark, there was nothing to hold you in and you could be tossed around like a pebble on a beach. There was a kind of restraining strap across the shoulders, otherwise when the aircraft went into a dive you would be squashed between the tanks.'

The rear gun was most often a Lewis MkIIIE, but some aircraft (usually those of the senior fliers) were fitted with a Vickers 'K' gun, which had a superior rate of fire to the Lewis and slightly less propensity to jam. 'The gunner had to be careful', said armourer Roy Stevens, 'as there were no 'stops' to prevent him hitting the fin or tail-planes as one did on the Bergen raid'[1]. The Skua was apparently never officially fitted with the Vickers gun but armourers and aircrews seem to have acquired their own. 'Compared to the Lewis it was like a Ford Model T next to a Lotus!' said 800 Squadron armourer Ron Jordan, adding 'but the Lewis was very reliable. I had considerable experience on the Lewis. I was ack-ack gunner on the station at Hatston and we had a double Lewis – didn't have a single stoppage.'

For carrier landings an A-frame arrestor hook was fitted between the aircraft's centre section and tail, and catapult attachment points were fitted, making the B-24 the first aircraft in British service to have these features designed in from the beginning.

The main wings were metal skinned, with two girder-type spars, and could be folded to lie along the fuselage with the leading edge uppermost. Dihedral was 1.2°. Hydraulically operated 'Zap' flaps were utilised, and these were one feature that would allow the Skua to become such a capable dive-bomber. The design was similar to conventional split flaps, but rather than hinging around a fixed point, the leading edge moved aft as the flap was extended. This enabled the flap/airbrake to be deployed without affecting trim.

The wings contained two Browning .303in No.4 MkII Browning machine guns in each mainplane with 600 rounds for each. The guns were controlled by armoured compressed air lines. Access to the guns and ammunition was by removable panels in the upper and lower surfaces of the wings. Access was considered good, but 're-arming with mainplanes folded was awkward', according to Roy Stevens.

Control surfaces were covered with fabric. The layout of the tail was similar to several de Havilland designs wherein the fin was set well ahead of the stabiliser to prevent the rudder being blanketed in a spin.

The engine was a Bristol Mercury 9 cylinder radial on the two prototypes, but replaced with a Bristol Perseus XII sleeve-valve 9 cylinder radial on the production aircraft. This was noted for its quiet running and, after early teething problems were resolved, considerable reliability and economy. It offered 830bhp for take-off, 745bhp for cruising and for five minutes, 905bhp. While cruising it would consume 60.3 gallons of fuel per hour.

The Skua was equipped with a GP (General Purpose or 'jeep') Wireless Telegraphy (W/T) set which consisted of a 1082 Receiver, a 1083 Transmitter and a R1110 beacon receiver (for detecting the aircraft carrier's revolving beacon). The W/T used an overhead aerial, but to make best use of the HF (High Frequency) equipment, a trailing aerial could be wound out by the TAG or Observer. Communication was only by Morse code, but the transmitter was also used as an amplifier to provide intercom between the front and rear cockpit, a vast improvement on the 'Gosport tubes' of previous FAA aircraft. Communication between aircraft in flight was basic or non-existent. 'All communication was by Morse – ship to aircraft or aircraft to ship,' said Lloyd Richards. 'There was not a lot of aircraft to aircraft communication – hand signal or Aldis lamp – not by radio'. The W/T set was tuned laboriously by fitting pairs of plugs (twenty pairs, one red plug and one green) into sockets, more or less by trial and error until the correct coil for a particular frequency was reached. Richards explained: 'You would get on your receiving frequency then back-tune the transmitter until you picked up your own signal. It was all done by hand, eye and making notes. When I was a boy, 13 years old, I built a radio which was more advanced than that unit in the Skua!'[2]

Navigation using the W/T equipment was also complex, requiring a great deal of skill on the part of the TAG. 'We didn't have D/F [Direction Finding] – we had a beacon radio,' said Lloyd Richards. 'The ship had D/F but that was not any good to us during war time... as it meant the fleet could have been found [by the enemy]. There was a little VHF beacon. On a vertical mast on the highest part of the ship there was a rotating cylinder, which would broadcast a screen every five seconds.' During war time it was by getting a 'fix' on this beacon that the crews would generally navigate back to the carrier. By timing whether the signal from the beacon came in at over or under a minute, the crews would be able to determine where the carrier was in relation to their own course. 'The beacon made one revolution per minute – initially we were issued with chronometers to time the signal, but they ran out with aircraft getting shot down, and they were very expensive. We subsequently used wristwatches,' said Richards. It is easy to criticise the Admiralty sticking for so long to the formula of two-seat fighters but given the lack of radar and even useful wireless telephony at this stage in the war a back-seater was completely necessary to help the pilot find his way. It would have been impossible for a pilot to operate the basic and demanding radio equipment and fly the aircraft.

From the cockpit

Opinions on the flying qualities of the Skua were, like most aircraft, varied. Some crews who were very well acquainted with the aircraft speak extremely fondly of its qualities. Cecil Filmer of 803 Squadron said: 'It was a very nice aircraft indeed, very easy to fly. It had very good front view, as the pilot sat so high up. It was a very gentle aircraft, I thought... It was a stable aircraft, in all respects'[3]. Of having to force land after the *Scharnhorst* raid, Filmer wrote: 'I really hated to lose my old Skua'.

Skua L2931 flies overhead in its factory pre-war silver colours, showing the fuselage and underside to good effect.

'I never had trouble with a Skua and as a rule they treated me well,' said Petty Officer H.A. Monk. 'I think it irked navy pilots that whilst the RAF was getting Hurricanes and Spitfires we got Skuas and Rocs, the main difference 100 mph and four .303 guns to eight for the RAF... (The) Skua was not a bad aeroplane to fly but being slow and under-gunned was a fighter pilot's dislike'[4].

Perhaps understandably, others were less keen. Later in the war Derrick Edwards flew Skuas on Fleet Requirements duties. 'We were warned when we took off, with the mountains to starboard, that if it did more than about 45° bank it would spin in. I don't know if that's true or not. I have to say though I didn't have any problems or accidents. It was what I describe as an old warhorse that had seen its day, and the examples we had were pretty worn out'[5].

Despite its lack of performance compared to more modern and powerful equipment, the Skua still managed to provoke some high-spirited flying from its youthful pilots. Derrick Edwards flew his Skua under both bridges crossing the narrow Menai strait between Wales and Anglesey. 'It was a TAG that dared me to do that, not once but twice,' he admitted. 'There was about a foot either side of the prop on top and bottom going under the road bridge, which is a lot lower than the rail bridge!' Not to be outdone, Sub Lieutenant Baldwin took a whole formation of Skuas between the rock known as 'The Old Man of Hoy' and the mainland. Observer Douglas Haskey recounts: 'that fellow Baldwin took a formation of us round Hoy and threaded the whole formation in between the Old Man and the cliffs. Now there's plenty of room for an aircraft – there isn't much room for a formation, and I still have a mental memory of looking up at the top of the Old Man!'

The tendency to spin was never entirely solved. According to one report, a new squadron suffered from three pilots crashing their new Skuas in one morning[6]. 'The Skua was not an aircraft you did aerobatics in,' said Derek Martin. 'Not unless you had plenty of altitude, seven, eight, nine thousand feet. If you got into a spin you were in trouble. That's why the Skua had a parachute in the tail. Aerodynamically the Skua was pretty bad'. Martin, a Midshipman pilot with 800 Squadron in 1940, summed up the feelings of many operational aircrews. 'As a fighter, the Skua was useless. It was far too slow to be a fighter. It could not really be compared with the Spitfire, which I flew later as the Seafire, nor the Hurricane which I did not fly. It was very good as a dive bomber provided you were unmolested by German fighters'[7].

The Roc was essentially similar to the Skua apart from the necessary modifications to allow the installation of the Boulton-Paul Type A turret. This involved widening of the rear fuselage and simplification of the lines under the rear cockpit, which was now flat and incorporated an entry hatch for the gunner.

The turret provided a radically different experience for the gunner than the Skua, and reports of this suggest some reasons why the Roc was not a success in practice. Former TAG Ken Sims wrote: '...the turret would not depress below the horizontal and this meant a nasty dead space under the tail. It also meant that during exercise firing at ground targets the pilot had to bank over. Surrounded by 4 Brownings and feed channels for the ammunition belts one couldn't see out much. There was a most odd sensation if the aircraft was turning and the turret was swung at the same time. One lost all sense of direction. There was a blanking off system to prevent shooting at your own tail. As the tail was quite large and the guns switched out in pairs there was a high probability that you only had two in action and a fair probability that you wouldn't have any at all. Not a very satisfactory defence arrangement. The turret could even dislodge from its mounting if the aircraft flew certain manoeuvres.'[8]

Pilot Officer Clarke's account of a battle between a Roc and a Heinkel He59 gives some idea of the limitations of trying to fight using a Roc:

'If only I had one front gun! Just one, and I'd be able to make a normal fighter attack. Instead, I was reduced to placing my aircraft in a ridiculously dangerous position where the other fellow had all the advantages... firing broadsides at him like one of Nelson's wooden walls! At 300 yards he looked terribly close.

'I lifted from nil feet (twice already my airscrew had flung spray over the wind-screen) to 20 feet and dipped my starboard wing, slowly easing on top rudder to keep a straight course. "FIRE!" I yelled. Once again the muzzle shock-wave drummed against my ears and the tracer twisted towards the enemy. Yes! We were hitting him! But there was only time for a quick burst. In a few seconds I found that the self-applied skid was dropping my starboard wing towards those ugly waves and I had to straighten out hurriedly - so rapidly that the final burst from our guns was fired into the broody sky."[9] Clarke, who later rose to the rank of Squadron Leader, claimed the Heinkel as 'damaged'.

Despite its performance shortcomings it seems the chief failings of the Roc were procedural, necessitating a counter-intuitive reversal in the relationship between pilot and gunner. Essentially the gunner was required to direct the pilot while also controlling the turret. This was an all but impossibly complex task, exacerbated by the often aloof relationship between officers and enlisted men. When the pilots were often the former and the gunners generally the latter, the customary lack of communication meant it was difficult for the aircraft to be used effectively. There needed to be 'a lot of training between pilot and gunner, and it was very difficult to do anything,' said Lloyd Richards. 'You would only need a little bit of wing drop and you'd be off target.' Armourer Ron Jordan concurred. 'The problem was that the air gunner controlled the aircraft, not the pilot.' The Roc was not entirely without its merits however, though even these draw at best qualified praise. 'The turret was a lovely piece of engineering, a real boy's delight,' said Ron Jordan. 'Useless on the aircraft though.'

---

1 Letter from Ron Stevens to Simon Partridge, 18th August 2006, reproduced by kind permission of Simon Partridge
2 L.G. Richards, in conversation with the author January 2007
3 C.H. Filmer in conversation with the author 11th November 2006
4 Letter from H A Monk to Ron Campbell 18th September 2001
5 Derrick Edwards in conversation with the author, 5th November 2006
6 Squadron Leader D.H. Clarke, The Shunned Skua, RAF Flying Review December 1961, p.35
7 Derek Martin in conversation with the author 5th November 2006
8 Ken Sims, Telegraphist Air Gunner, draft manuscript pp. 20-21
9 Squadron Leader D.H. Clarke, RAF Flying Review, October 1961, p.40

Conclusion

It would be easy to categorise the Skua and Roc as aircraft that were in service in the early part of the Second World War that were found to be totally outclassed despite being relatively new, a consequence of the lighting pace of aircraft development in the years leading up to war. Like the Fairey Battle or the Morane-Saulnier MS.406, the Skua's history is also characterised by desperate rearguard actions or hopeless counter-attacks against the German domination of Europe.

Nevertheless, despite limitations such as the lack of a proper method of bomb-aiming[1], and an inability to carry a larger bomb than 500lb, the Skua's short career had already proved it to be, in the words of Major Partridge, a 'first-class dive bomber'. The attack on Bergen proved that with a measure of surprise (or adequate fighter cover) attacks on lightly armoured ships could be accomplished with devastating effects. Many more dive bombing attacks followed over Norway, France, the Mediterranean and the Channel Islands. Though the majority of these missions have received little attention, the intensive use of the Skua as a strike aircraft against merchant shipping, military and industrial targets tells how valuable this aircraft was found to be.

As a dive bomber, though it suffered its share of losses, the Skua had sufficient performance to prevent disastrous attrition of the nature of the German Ju87 squadrons when they were forced to go up against modern fighters. Indeed, for a too-slow, too heavy aircraft, the Skua exceeded expectations as a bomber destroyer, and with the right tactics and experienced crews, the Skua actually fulfilled its fleet-fighter design brief. Despite being outnumbered and never enjoying air superiority, the FAA's Skuas made an invaluable contribution to the Norwegian campaign and saved many of the Allies involved from the consequences of unopposed German bombing. While on paper looking inferior even to the Sea Gladiator in some respects, its endurance made it an ideal machine for long range fighter patrols over land and sea, maintaining standing cover over land forces, escorting strikes and providing close support. That the Allied ground forces in Norway did not suffer the fate of the Polish, Belgian and Dutch armies is in part a testament to the fact that the Skua was a more capable fighter than the Allies had a right to expect. Norway, however, made it clear that the FAA could not rely on a 'fighter' that was designed to stave off fleet shadowers and torpedo bombers – it needed an aircraft that could live with the enemy's best land-based interceptors.

It is perhaps unfortunate that early impressions of the Skua stuck, when later experience showed these characteristics in a different light Originally thought to be too big for a fighter, the Skua was much lighter and smaller than aircraft which came after it, even single seaters such as the Grumman Hellcat. For a 'modern' monoplane the Skua had generally good deck characteristics – and was a breeze compared to later Seafires and Corsairs.

Perhaps tellingly, the Skua is most often chastised for its low speed and poor rate of climb, hardly fair when its replacement, the Fairey Fulmar, was barely 20mph faster and had a comparable rate of climb. Most importantly, replacing the Skua with Fulmars and Sea Hurricanes all but ended the Navy's ability to dive-bomb.

There were never enough Skuas to make the kind of difference the aircraft might have been capable of in the strike role, and there will always be significant questions over the contribution it could have made. To have faced more modern opposition in theatres such as the Pacific would possibly have been a senseless waste of aircraft and crews. Alternatively, the experience of 1940 and early 1941 could have enabled the Fleet Air Arm to develop dive bombing as effectively as the US and Japanese navies did. Perhaps a properly used and developed Skua could have been the RN's Douglas SBD Dauntless - potentially one of the outstanding naval strike aircraft of the war. That the Vice Admiral Commanding Orkneys and Shetlands could refer to a Skua squadron as 'the finest dive bombers in the world' shows the regard these aircraft and their crews had earned.

These men were not heroes in the sense of aerial Achilles or Sir Gawains hunting for glory and demonstrating their prowess – they were men who had a job to do and did it. It just so happened that this job was incredibly difficult and dangerous, and utterly necessary. The Skua was not the kindest aircraft to its crews, uncomfortable, lightly armoured and relatively ponderous. It was, however, a powerful weapon and that it engendered loyalty, even affection, from the men who crewed it, speaks volumes for its worth. Ultimately, the Skua's story is one of unrecognised achievements, a machine that was greater than the sum of its parts – and a glimpse of how things might have been different for the FAA between 1941 and 1944.

The remains of Skua L2940 as discovered by a Norwegian army ski patrol. The aircraft was force landed by Captain R.T. Partridge and Lieutenant R. Bostock on the 27th April 1940 after a battle with a Heinkel He111. They set fire to the fuel tanks to prevent sensitive material falling into German hands. (Fleet Air Arm Museum)

---

1   See Peter C. Smith, Skua!, chapter 3 'The Saga of the Dive Bomb Sight'

Blackburn Skua data table

Length (prototype)	33' 2 ¼"	10.12m
Length (production)	35'7"	10.85m
Span	46'2"	14.08m
Width folded	15'6"	4.72m
Height	12'6"	3.81m
Undercarriage track	9'7"	2.92m
Dihedral	1.2°	
Empty weight	5,496lb	2,489.69kg
Combat weight (bomber)	8,204.5lb	3,716.64kg
Combat weight (fighter)	8105.5lb	3671.79kg
Maximum speed	225mph (at 6,500ft)	362km/h
Cruising speed	187mph	301km/h
Economic cruise	114mph	183km/h
Service ceiling	20,200ft	6,157m
Rate of climb	1,580ft/min	481.6m/min
Endurance	4 hours 20 minutes, 435 miles	700km
Fuel capacity	145 gallons	662l
Engine	Bristol Perseus XII	
Maximum power	905 bhp	675 kW
Take-off power	830 bhp	619 kW
Cruising power	745 bhp	555 kW

Blackburn Roc data table

Length	35'7"	10.85m
Span	46'0"	14.03m
Width folded	15'6"	4.72m
Height	12'1"	3.68m
Undercarriage track	9'7"	2.92m
Dihedral	2°	
Empty weight	6,124lb	2,774.17kg
Combat weight	8,670lb	3,927.51kg
Maximum speed	223mph (at 10,000ft)	359km/h
Cruising speed	135mph	217km/h
Service ceiling	18,000ft	5,486m
Rate of climb	1,500ft/min	457m/min
Endurance	2 hours 30 minutes	
Engine	Bristol Perseus XII	
Maximum power	905 bhp	675 kW
Take-off power	830 bhp	619 kW
Cruising power	745 bhp	555 kW

Fuselage & Engine

A classic photograph of a Skua in full dive-bombing trim, with flaps at full 80° extension. L2883 was from the first batch of 69 Skuas and was delivered to 803 Squadron in December 1938. (Stratus collection)

L2886 from the rear, January 1939. The rear gunner's canopy has been pivoted fully forwards to allow maximum visibility and field of fire. (BAE Systems)

The nose of a production Skua. The cooling gills are open fully and the many fastenings of the removable cowling panels are clearly in evidence. From the firewall (represented by the panel line running circumferentially around the fuselage) to the engine mount, the nose was constructed of a tubular steel structure covered by unstressed alloy panels. The vent at the top of the fuselage is the port oil-cooler outlet, usually covered by a fairing. (BAE Systems)

A head-on view of the Skua nose. The de Havilland airscrew was a metal, two-pitch item, the hub covered by a small spinner. The two 'nostrils' are the oil cooler intakes. The catapult attachment points can be seen under the centre section – the Skua was the first British aircraft designed with these features from the beginning. (BAE Systems)

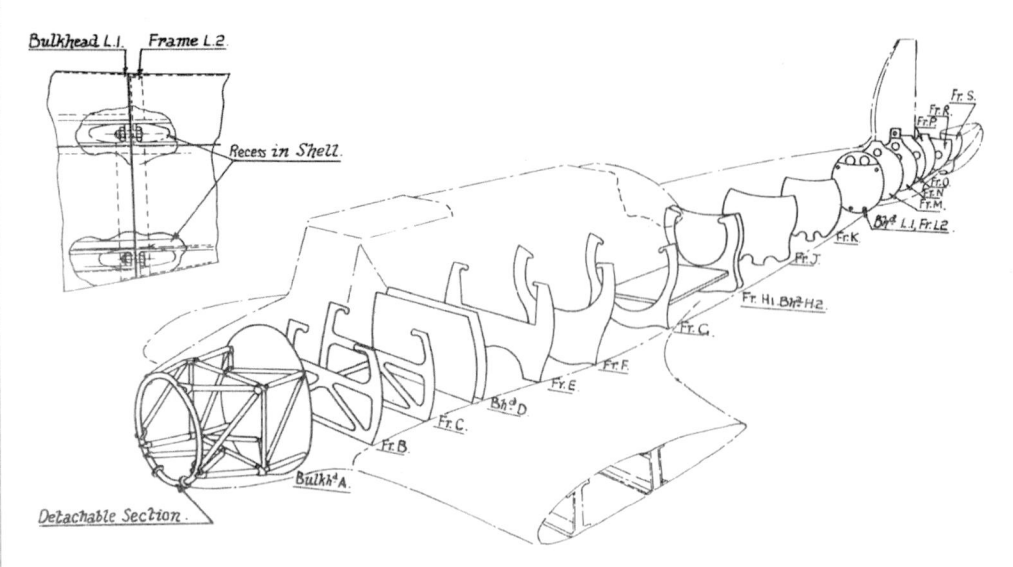

Above: The layout of the frames in the Skua's fuselage, showing the position of the bomb recess (Frame E) and the point where the rear fuselage can be detached (Bulkhead L.1). The inset shows the attachment for the rear fuselage and tail. Note the tubular engine mount at the nose. (Air Ministry).

Below: The construction of the tail, with aluminium ribs and stringers. The fin and tail plane are covered with Alclad riveted to the structure, while rudder and elevators are fabric-covered. Note trim and balance tabs on the trailing edges. (Air Ministry)

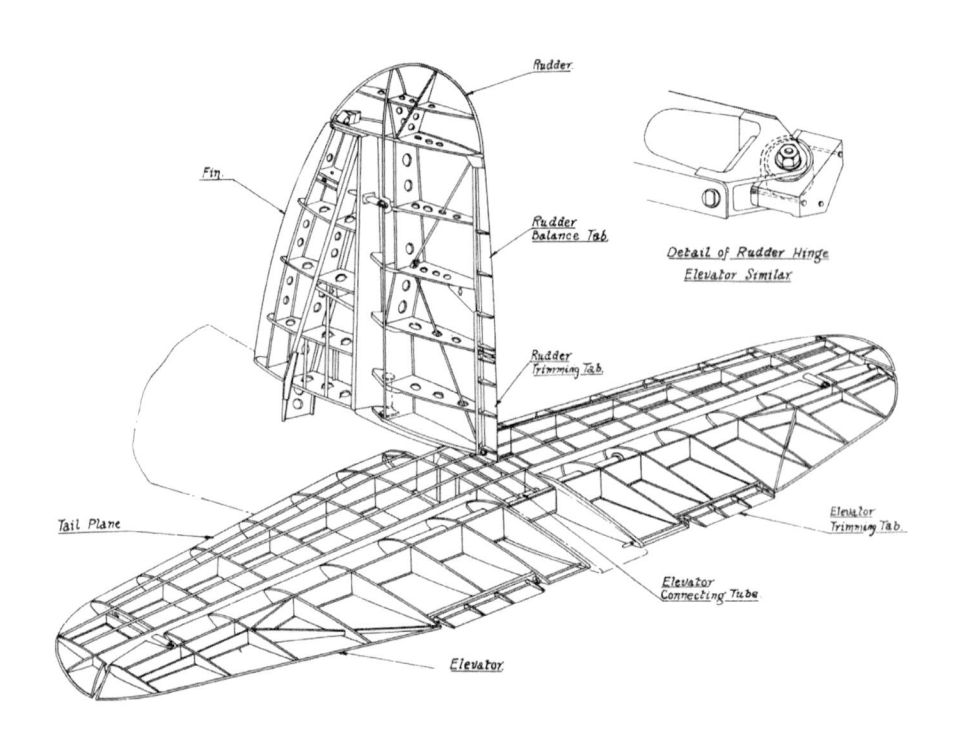

Top: Roc L3147 photographed in June 1941. Note the modification to the early war 'temperate sea scheme' in which the demarcation line for the upper camouflage has been extended down the side of the fuselage for most of its length, but retains the high demarcation at the nose and tail. The fin flash has been reduced to half-height. (Central Press Photographs, courtesy of BAE Systems Brough Heritage)
Bottom: Three all-silver Skuas taxying at a grass aerodrome before the outbreak of war. The nearest two aircraft appear to have their flaps set in the take-off position of 30°, and all have light-series bomb racks fitted. (Stratus collection)

A detail picture of the tubular engine mount's construction. This was formed from steel tubes with cast attachments at either end to allow them to be bolted together to form a spaceframe. This arrangement tended to mean the engine was often torn from the firewall in crashes. (BAE Systems)

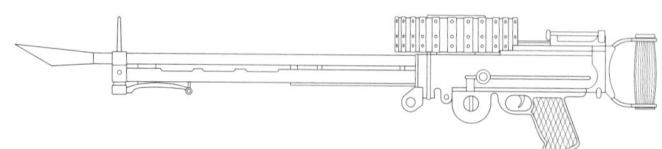

A rare shot of the Fairey pillar machine gun mounting in the Skua rear cockpit. When the gun was not in use the barrel rested in the recess that can be seen in the rear fuselage, and the pivoting mounting allowed the gun to be swung upwards and back into a position to cover the rear of the aircraft. The gun pictured is a Lewis MkIIIE, but many crews unofficially procured Vickers 'K' Gas Operated machine guns. The rear canopy had to be swung forward to allow the gun to be operated. (BAE Systems)

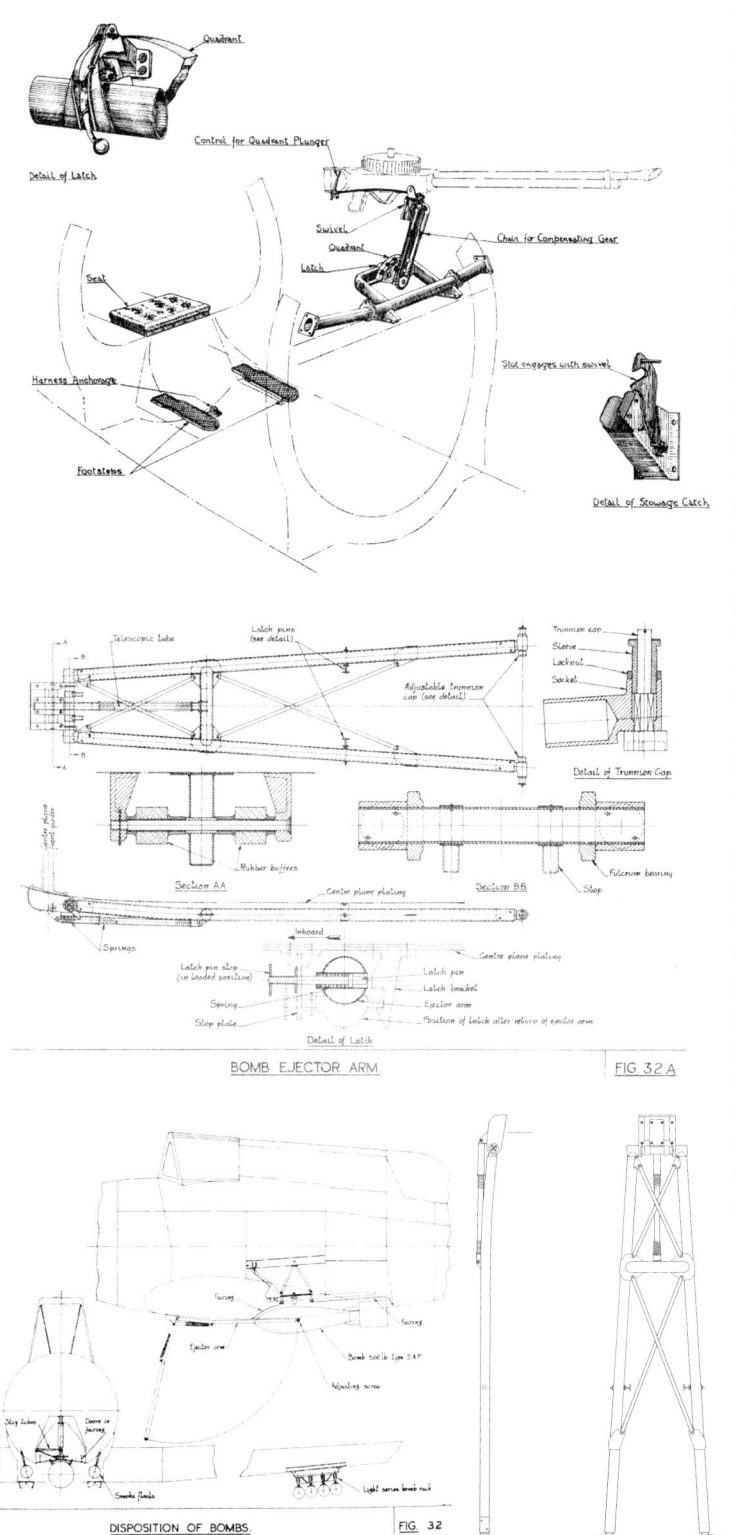

Top: The layout of the Skua rear cockpit showing the Fairey pillar mounting for the Lewis gun and the gunner's seat, which was a thin pad on top of the inner face of the bomb recess, with foot rests for stability. The detail shows the latch that locked the gun in the upper position when the pillar was swung backwards and upwards. (Air Ministry)

Middle: The arm used to swing the central bomb out of the Skua's under-fuselage recess and clear of the propeller arc when dive-bombing. It had adjustable trunnions to accept a range of bombs from the 100lb anti-submarine to the 500lb armour-piercing. (Air Ministry)

Lower, left: The Skua's bomb mounting - a bomb rack was fitted deep within the fuselage in the centre section, allowing a bomb to be carried partially recessed into the fuselage for drag reduction. The Skua and Roc could also carry 'Light Series' bomb racks under each wing, with 20lb, 40lb or practice bombs. (Air Ministry)

Three views of the the air cleaner from Skua L2872, which was returned to Blackburns for trial modifications. This intake provided air for the carburettor, and was covered by a fairing. (BAE Systems)

Below: *The two-pitch propeller fitted to the Skua. This was a de Havilland unit (licence-built to a Hamilton Standard design) with steel blades. Most Skuas and Rocs fitted a small aluminium spinner. (Air Ministry)*

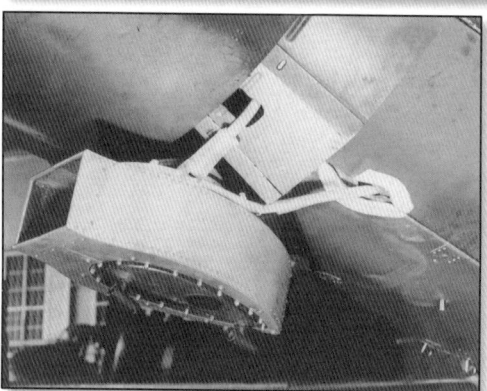

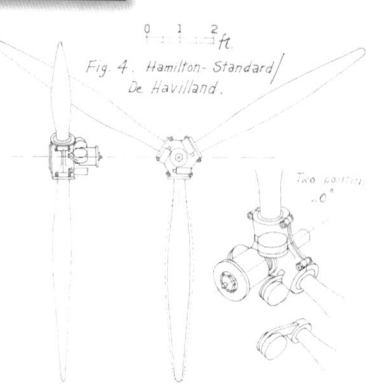

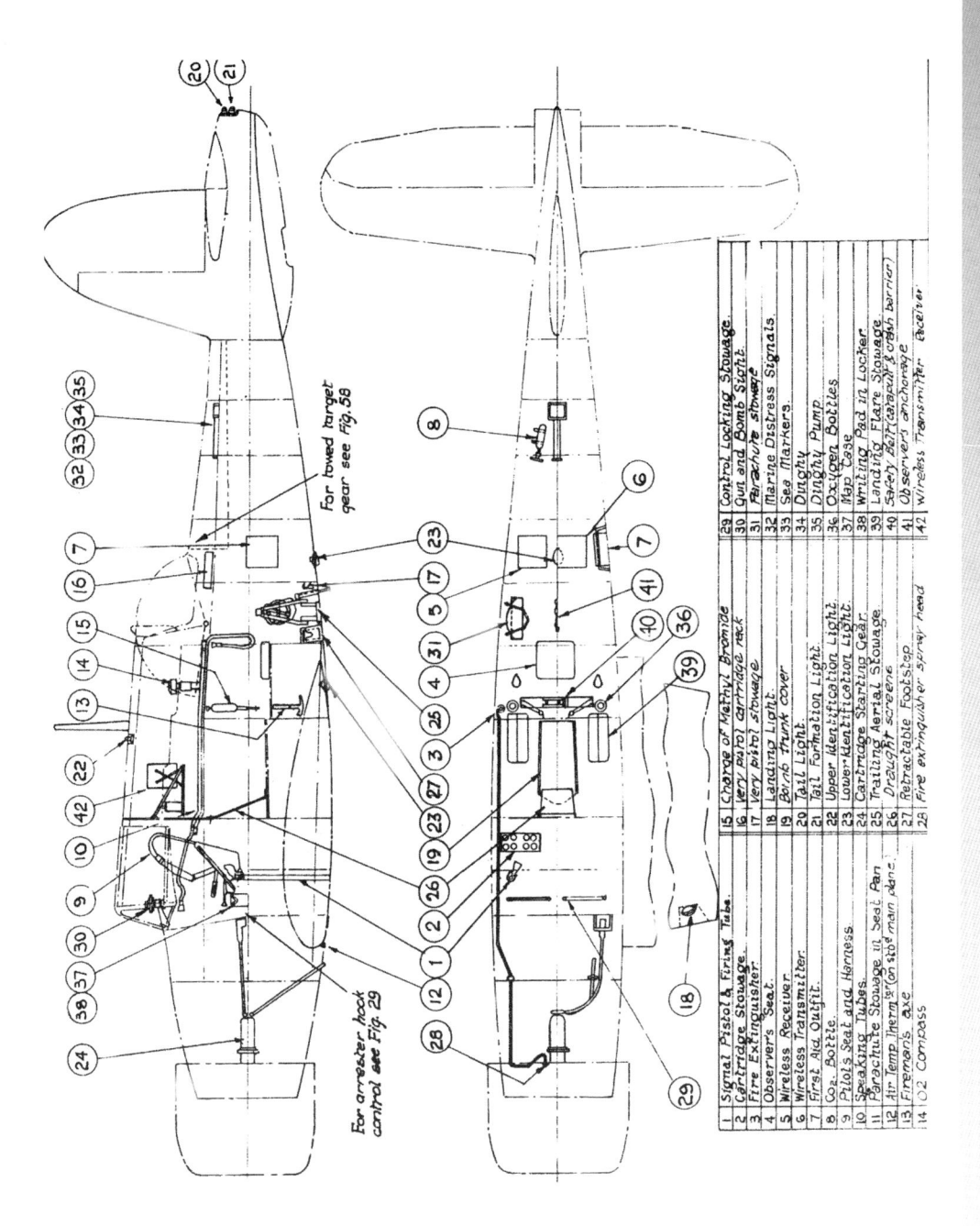

Diagram showing the layout of the Skua's major equipment. (Air Ministry)

#	Item	#	Item
1	Signal Pistol & Firing Tubes	22	Upper Identification Light
2	Cartridge Stowage	23	Lower Identification Light
3	Fire Extinguisher	24	Cartridge Starting Gear
4	Observer's Seat	25	Trailing Aerial Stowage
5	Wireless Receiver	26	Draught screens
6	Wireless Transmitter	27	Retractable Footstep
7	First Aid Outfit	28	Fire extinguisher spray head
8	CO_2 Bottle	29	Control Locking Stowage
9	Pilot's Seat and Harness	30	Gun and Bomb Sight
10	Speaking Tubes	31	Parachute stowage
11	Parachute Stowage in Seat Pan	32	Marine Distress Signals
12	Air Temp Thermr (on side of main plane)	33	Sea Markers
13	Fireman's axe	34	Dinghy
14	O_2 Compass	35	Dinghy Pump
15	Charge of Methyl Bromide	36	Oxygen Bottles
16	Very pistol cartridge rack	37	Map Case
17	Very pistol stowage	38	Writing Pad in Locker
18	Landing Light	39	Landing Flare Stowage
19	Bomb Trunk cover	40	Safety Belt (catapult) & crash barrier
20	Tail Light	41	Observer's anchorage
21	Tail Formation Light	42	Wireless Transmitter Receiver

Blackburn Skua & Roc

Cockpit & Canopy

The rear cockpit of the Skua, which was little more than the empty interior of the aircraft. The top of the bomb recess can be seen between and behind the two main, non-self sealing, fuel tanks (in the foreground on either side) which formed the rear gunner's seat. The observer's morse key can be seen to the left of the picture, above the fuel tank. The foremost fuselage frame visible in the picture extends to the roof of the cockpit for greater crew protection. (BAE Systems)

Flight Lieutenant Thompson in the cockpit of Roc L3147 in June 1941. Note the reflector gunsight – although the Roc had no forward facing armament, the turret could be fixed in the forward position, firing above the propeller arc, and control of the guns transferred to the pilot. (BAE Systems)

Contemporary photograph of the front cockpit of the Skua. The instrument panel was the standard blind flying panel, leaving little room for the other instruments which are arranged either side of the pilot's legs. A large compass can be seen in the middle of the floor. The large lever to the right of the seat was very effective for jacking the pilot up to a considerable height to give the best possible view for carrier landing. The reflector gunsight virtually fills the almost-vertical windshield. (BAE Systems)

Diagram showing the flight controls for the Skua and Roc. These operated on a pull-pull system with wires in a closed loop. The control column moved fore-and-aft in its entirety for pitch control, while the top part only pivoted for roll control. A standard spade grip carried gun and camera buttons, and wheel brake lever.

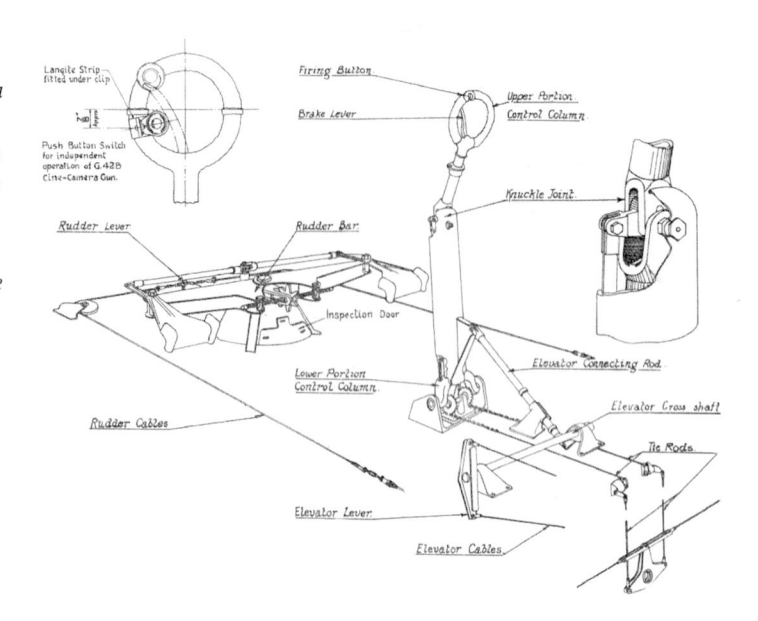

Note: For further details on the Boulton Paul Mk.II turret, see the MMP book on the Boulton Paul Defiant.

L2951 from 771 NAS meets its end after nosing over at RNAS Twatt on Orkney, October 1942 while on second-line duties. The state of wear and tear that characterised the hard-used training and fleet requirements Skuas at this stage in the war is much in evidence. (Fleet Air Arm Museum)

Wing

L2886, one of the early production aircraft, demonstrating flaps in the fully extended position at the Blackburn factory in January 1939. Note how the leading edge has drawn backwards as the flap extended. Also in evidence are the doors that cover the smoke float compartments, and the numerous small inspection hatches along the rear fuselage. L2886 was issued to 803 Squadron at Worthy Down in January 1939. (BAE Systems)

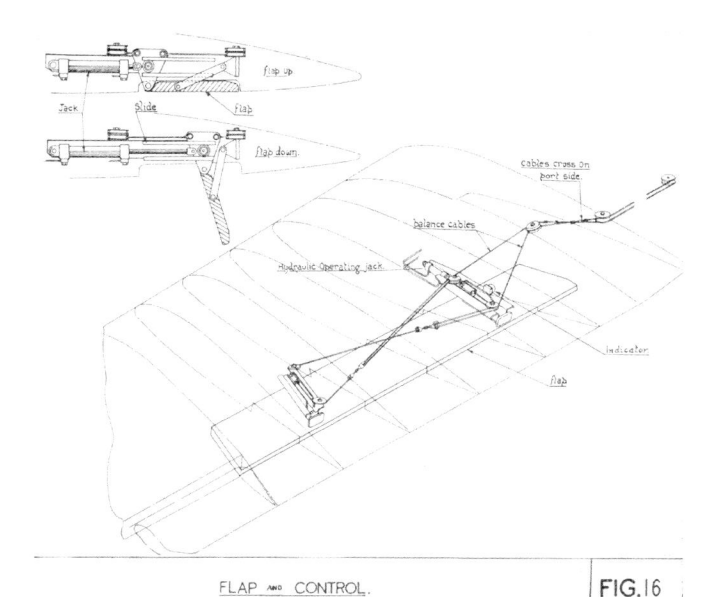

The Skua's powerful flaps/dive brakes, which contributed significantly to the aircraft's success as a dive bomber. The flaps were powered by a combination of hydraulic rams and a system of wires. The flaps resembled conventional split flaps, but the diagram shows how a sliding rack allowed the leading edge to move backwards as the flap extended. This helped the aircraft maintain the same trim in pitch as the flaps were deployed.

FLAP AND CONTROL. FIG.16

Undercarriage

A close-up of the wing-fold mechanism on K5179, which remained the same for production aircraft. Latch pins are placed in the substantial rings along the top of the wing former to lock the wing in the unfolded position. Folding and unfolding is manual. Note how the undercarriage is located on the centre section but folds into the out section when retracted. (BAE Systems)

The lubrication diagram from the Skua's Air Publication shows the design of the oleo strut and its retraction arms.

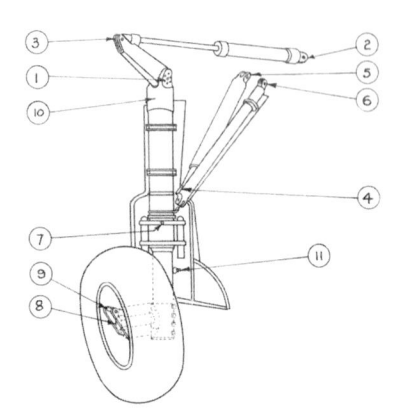

Nº	Description	Nº of Points	Lubrication
1	Oleo Strut Top Hinge Pin	1	
2	Inboard Jack Connection	2	
3	Retracting Lever Joint	2	
4	Telescopic Strut Bottom Joint	1	
5	Telescopic Strut Top Joint	1	
6	Radius Arm Top Joint	1	
7	Oleo Strut Gland	1	
8	Undercarriage Wheel Hub Bearing	1	
9	Stirrup Roller Bearings	1	
10	Oleo Strut Cylinder	1	
11	Indicator Plunger	1	

Note: The Nº of Points refer to one undercarriage unit only.

● Oil, Lubricating, Anti-freezing, D.T.D 201 (Stores Ref 34A/55 & 56)
■ Grease, Anti-freezing, D.T.D. 143 B (Stores Ref 34A/49)
◉ Oil, Anti-freezing, D.T.D. 44 B (Stores Ref 34A/43 & 46)

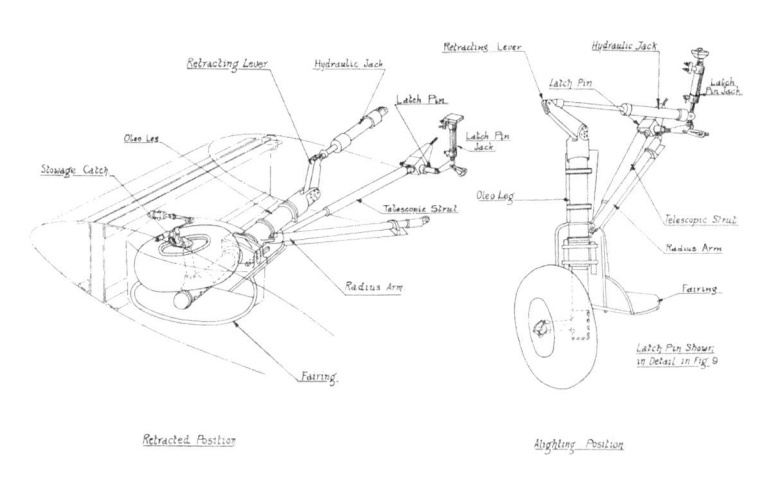

The Skua and Roc's undercarriage, in both extended and retracted positions. The oleo-strut units retracted outwards into the wing powered by hydraulic jacks. Note on the diagram a folding fairing is shown which covers the wheel when retracted - this was deleted for production models. Tyres are low-pressure Dunlops.

The Skua tailwheel assembly. Note the black painted scissor joint assembly which is 'mod 152', a friction damper to reduce shimmy. The aircraft is the Brough trials and modifications machine L2872. . (BAE Systems)

Flight Lieutenant Thompson waves away the chocks in Roc L3147. The large, low pressure tyres were specified to improve landings on aircraft carriers, but also improved the aircraft's ground handling on grass airfields. (BAE Systems)

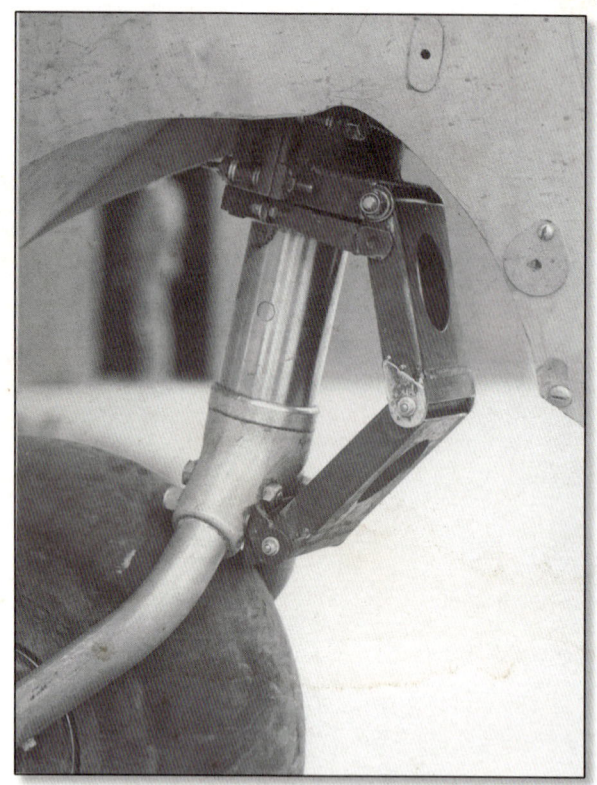

The tail fin of the wreck of Skua L2940 in the Fleet Air Arm Museum. The remains of the camouflage paint can be seen on the top of the fuselage, while the code letter 'A' is pencilled on the fin. (Author)

This picture of the remains of L2940 shows the recess in the rear fuselage for an emergency dinghy. (Author)

Another photograph of the tail of L2940 - note the serial on the rear fuselage which survived decades submerged in a Norwegian lake. (Author)

The nose, propeller, engine and engine mounting of Skua L2940 in the Fleet Air Arm Museum. The Perseus engine can clearly be seen, and the pipes that connect the cylinders to the exhaust collector ring at the front of the nose. The heat that the collector ring was subjected to appears to have hastened rusting in places. (Author)

The port side undercarriage leg of Skua L2940, protruding from the wing - the white paint on the underside of the wing (the port wing's underside is black) can still be seen after 67 years. (Author)

The rear fuselage of L2940 showing the interior structure of stringers and frames. (Author)

A close up of the interior structure of Skua L2940 where it is displayed at the Fleet Air Arm Museum. (Author)

A close-up of L2940's propeller spinner, also showing the reduction gear casing. (Author)

Stencils on L2940's port wing. These can clearly be seen despite 35 years submerged beneath Lake Grotli where the Skua force landed in 1940. (Author)

The underside of Skua L2940's port wing. Note the flap which is slightly extended, showing how the leading edge moved aft as the angle of the flap increased. (Author)

The port wing of L2940 showing some remnants of the extra-dark-sea-grey/dark-slate-grey upper surface camouflage. Note the closely-spaced lines of laboriously applied flush rivets - the Skua was heavily constructed to withstand the stresses of dive bombing. (Author)

Detail of the broken starboard wing-root of Skua L2940. (Author)

Lieutenant C.H. Filmer shot down a Heinkel He111 on the 26th of April 1940, but was forced to ditch near Ålesund. The Skua was recovered by British forces (though it had lost its engine in the impact) and colour film of the recovery was taken by a Norwegian civilian. (Kjell Holm, via Øyvind Lamo)

Bottom: *An overall view of L2991 following its recovery at Ålesund on the 26th April 1940. Note the single letter 'Q' on the tail fin, as carrier air group letters and numbers had been deleted by this time. Many Skuas retained the night/white wing undersides that were used as an identification device for British aircraft operating from UK land bases. Flaps are still deployed. (Kjell Holm, via Øyvind Lamo)*

The outer wing root and fuselage side of L2991. The wing root appears to be painted a blue-grey, possibly sky grey.

Close-up of L2991's Type-A fuselage roundel, in darker 'wartime' colours.

The starboard undercarriage leg of L2991 following its force landing on water near Ålesund. The 'night' black underside paint appears to have chipped badly through to the sky grey underneath, possibly during the ditching. (Kjell Holm, via Øyvind Lamo)

Top and middle:
The metal framed Perspex of the rear canopy, which could be swung back into the cockpit to allow the rear gun to be deployed and give a clear field of fire. The canopy appears to have been penetrated by a single bullet. TAG Kenneth Baldwin was killed during an attack on a Heinkel He111 before the Skua ditched. (Kjell Holm, via Øyvind Lamo)

L2991's cockpit. The 'blind flying panel' consisting of the six main instruments appears to have been removed. The control column, with its brass gun button, and broken gunsight can clearly be seen. (Kjell Holm, via Øyvind Lamo)

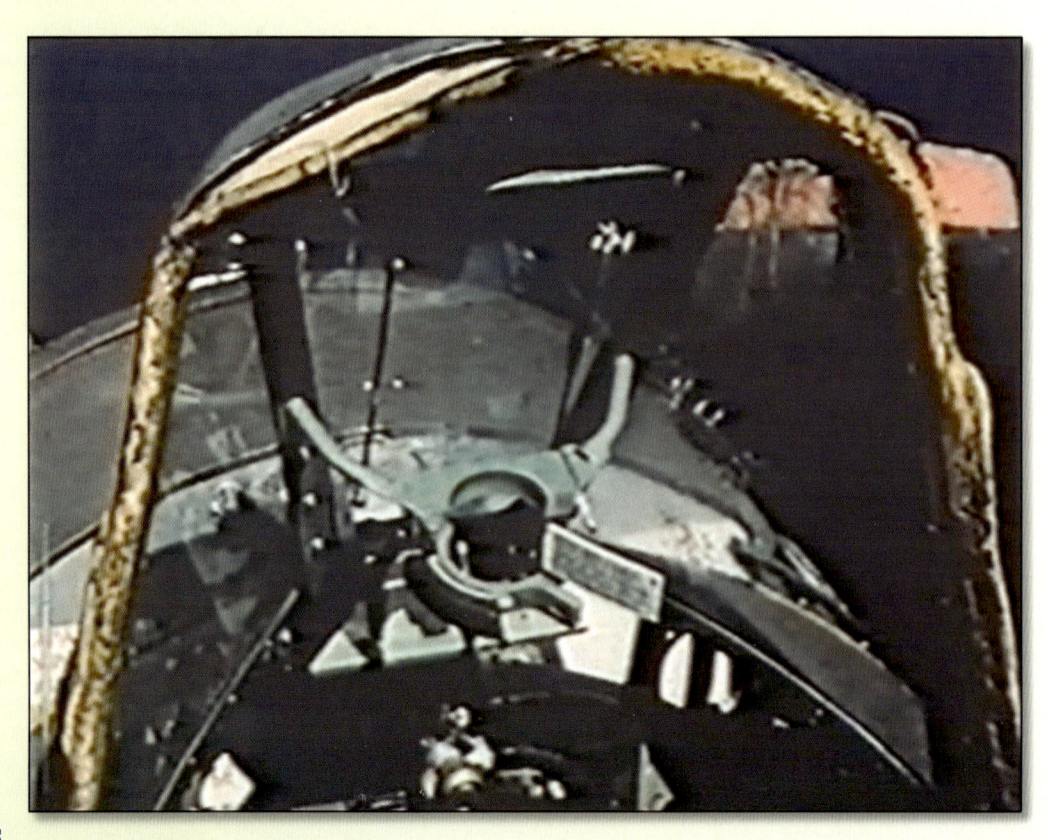

Skua L2991 at Ålesund. Note the pale camouflage colours and the stencil on the rudder. (Kjell Holm, via Øyvind Lamo)

The cockpit section reconstructed from a number of crashed Skuas by the Norsk Luftfartmuseum Bodo. Note the large compass between the pilot's feet and the lack of armour protection for the pilot. (Author)

A close-up of the main instrument panel which was the standard 'blind-flying panel' used by all RAF and FAA single-seat aircraft of the time. The instruments are air-speed indicator, artificial horizon, rate of climb indicator, altimeter, gyro compass and fuel gauge. (Author)

The port side instrument panel of the reconstructed Skua cockpit, with (from the bottom) rudder/elevator trim indicator, brake pressure indicator, flap indicator and electric power indicator. (Author)

A close-up of the nose art applied to the NLM Bodø's reconstructed Skua cockpit. The nose art is new, but based on that worn on Skua L2963 which was lost on the raid on the Scharnhorst in June 1940. (Author)

The starboard side instrument panel of the cockpit reconstruction, showing (from the bottom) starboard and port fuel gauges, primer switch cock, forward fuel gauge and oxygen regulator. (Author)

Floor-mounted compass and rudder bar from the reconstructed Skua cockpit. (Author)

The rear of the Skua's artificial horizon indicator, stencilled with 'Do not jar, handle like eggs'. (Author)

The oil tank from the NLM Bodo's Skua cockpit reconstruction. Note how the top of the tank forms the outer skin of the fuselage. The bullet hole is original. (Author)

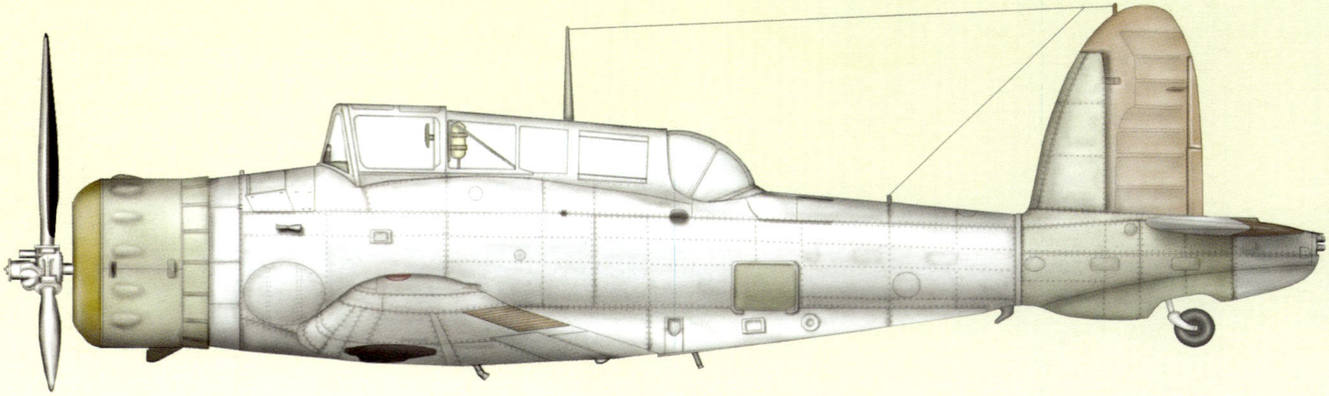

Above: Skua K5178 was the first prototype aircraft and retrospectively designated Skua MkI. Although substantially similar to the production MkII, the aircraft had a shorter nose and used a Bristol Mercury radial which altered the forward lines considerably, and wingtips were not upturned as on later versions. The aircraft first appeared unfinished, with no markings and apparently in a mix of primer and bare metal.
Below: K5178 after the first flight in February 1937. By this time the aircraft had been painted, and it is believed that the colour scheme was pale green (as shown here), but has also been suggested to be blue or grey. Upper wing surfaces and tail surfaces were silver or bare metal.

Above: Skua K5178 after June 1937 after the figure 8 was added to the rear fuselage for the 'new types park' at the Hendon air display. Photographs of the aircraft at this time show a distinct tonal difference between the middle fuselage, and the cowling and rear of the aircraft, which is not apparent in earlier photographs. Parts of the aircraft may have been repainted before the display.
Below: Second prototype K5179 benefited from lessons learned with K5178. The aircraft appears to have worn two slightly different colour schemes in its life, the first possibly all over bare metal and the second a duller silver. In the second of these, the rudder shows distinct tonal differences from the rest of the aircraft, suggesting that control surfaces were not repainted.

Blackburn Skua & Roc

143

Above: A number of photographs from Eastleigh in late 1939 and early 1940 show Skuas such as this one in an intriguing all-black scheme. The purpose of the scheme is unknown, though Eastleigh was home to at least two second-line Skua squadrons at this time. The paintwork appears to have suffered very badly from wear and chipping and resembles the colour known as 'special night' used for night fighters and bombers, which had a very matt finish that degraded easily. The identities of the black Skuas are unknown.

Below: L2867 was the first production Skua and was used for a range of development work to prepare the Skua for service use in late 1938 and early 1939. This included the radio equipment, target towing and accelerator use, both on land at the RAE and later at sea with HMS Courageous.

Above: Skua L2887 was one of the first batch and among the earliest to be issued to 803 Squadron - which lost no time in adorning its aircraft in the colourful fuselage bands common to Ark Royal based aircraft. Tail stripes were also worn by aircraft flown by Flight leaders. L2887 survived the Skua's frontline service, but was lost in a crash at Itchen Abbas in 1941.

Below: Skua L2889 was among the first Skuas to be issued to squadron service and joined 803 NAS in late 1938 or early 1939. Before the war 803 NAS used 'A7' as their squadron code, which later changed to 'A8'. L2889 was still in use by 803 Squadron during the Norwegian campaign and it is possible that this airframe was used by 803's commanding officer, Lieutenant Commander John Casson

Blackburn Skua & Roc

145

Skua L2925, which was shot down on the 14th May 1940 while being flown by Lieutenant William Paulet Lucy. Lucy was the Fleet Air Arm's first 'ace' with seven shared victories, and the Distinguished Service Order after leading the squadron in the sinking of the Königsberg on the 10th April 1940. Lucy and his observer, Lieutenant Michael Hanson, were killed.
Bottom: *Skua L2928 was reputed to be one of the original aircraft to form 801 Squadron at Donibristle in April 1939, but most known photographs show the aircraft in the scheme worn by Fleet Air Arm advanced trainers - extra dark sea grey and dark slate grey upper surfaces (with a low demarcation unlike the earlier naval scheme) and sky undersides. This suggests the aircraft passed to a second-line squadron.*

Above: *While Ark Royal was en route to the Mediterranean, the ship's Skuas took part in filming for the Ealing Studios picture 'Ships with Wings'. Stills from the film show some interesting details including this Skua A6K which may have been Lieutenant Spurway's L2933. Interpretation of the stills, along with the recollections of personnel, suggest that some Skuas may have had Azure blue undersides for a short time. Serials were painted out during the filming.*
Below: *Skua L2940 of 800 Squadron as flown by Captain Partridge RM over Norway on the 27th April 1940. Captain Partridge shot down a Heinkel He111 but was forced to ditch near Grotli and set fire to it before he and his Observer, Lieutenant Bostock, walked to safety. Partridge had been using L2940 for less than week. The remains were recovered in 1975 and now reside in the Fleet Air Arm Museum.*

Blackburn Skua & Roc

147

Above: Skua L2942 was operated by 801 Squadron during its campaign of 'nuisance' raids over Norway in the second half of 1940. L2942 was flown by Sub-Lieutenant B.F. Wigginton and K.R. King on a raid to Trondheim on the 22nd September 1940. The crew could not find the target and could not raise HMS Furious for a return bearing, so they ditched in Sweden and were interned for a year. Note the non-standard sloping fin flash and unusual serial typeface. Areas of Dark Slate Grey appear to have been repainted.

Below: Skua L2955 'Q' of 803 Squadron, which was flown by Sub-Lieutenant Dick Bartlett and Naval Airman Lloyd Richards on the raid against the Scharnhorst on June 13th 1940. The aircraft was force-landed South of Trondheim after sustaining damage, and the crew set it on fire. The unusual serif typeface of the serial suggests the aircraft had been transferred from 801 Squadron.

Above: L2963 as it appeared on the raid against the Scharnhorst on June the 13th 1940. The aircraft was flown by Lieutenant C.H. Filmer and Midshipman Thomas Anthony McKee of 803 Squadron on the raid in which eight of 15 Skuas were lost. Filmer ditched L2963 after being repeatedly attacked by a Messerschmitt Bf110. The aircraft was recovered by German forces.
Below: L2963 early in the Norwegian campaign when flown on occasion by Lieutenant William Paulet Lucy, in command of 803 Squadron.

Blackburn Skua & Roc

149

Blackburn Skua & Roc

Above: Skua L2987 was one of those assigned to escort Hurricanes to Malta on the 17th November 1940, but due to the long range and other problems, fewer than half the aircraft reached the island. L2987 ran low on fuel and was forced to ditch by Sicily. Photographs show the aircraft to have had an unusual colour scheme with a serif serial number and no code letter. Anecdotal evidence suggests that some Mediterranean theatre Skuas may have gained blue undersides, which could have been Azure.

Below: Skua L2991 was flown by Lieutenant C.H. Filmer and Petty Officer K.G. Baldwin of 803 Squadron on the 26th April 1940 when they shot down a Heinkel He111 but were hit by return fire and forced to ditch. Baldwin was killed but Filmer put the aircraft down near Ålesund where it was recovered to shore by British forces and later destroyed.

150

Above: Skua L3007 was one of the first machines of the final batch of Skuas, and was used to test a black and yellow striped colour scheme that later became standard for all British target tugs. L3007 did not become a target tug itself but later served with 803 Squadron in the Mediterranean. The aircraft is often reported as having worn an experimental red and white striped scheme for ditching trials, but no evidence exists to show if these colours were actually applied..
Below: Skua L3011 was issued to 806 Squadron, the fourth and final frontline Skua unit, where it gained these colours. This squadron apparently kept the full three figure tail code at a time when other squadrons had removed all but the individual aircraft letter, and used a large, square typeface for this. The squadron used Type B roundels on the fuselage when others used Type A. The squadron dive bombed targets in Norway on several occasions in May 1940.

Blackburn Skua & Roc

151

Above: Skua L3047 was assigned to 800 Squadron in the second half of the Norwegian campaign. It was flown on the raid against the Scharnhorst by Midshipman Derek Martin, who had joined the squadron in May, and Leading Airman W.J. Tremeer. L3047 was in the rearmost flight as the squadron approached Trondheim and was bounced by Messerschmitt Bf110s. The controls were shot away and Tremeer killed by gunfire. Martin bailed out and was captured.
Below: Lieutenant Callingham's Skua L3048, which ran low on fuel after dive bombing Trondheim harbour with 803 Squadron on the 25th April 1940. Callingham set the aircraft down almost undamaged on Spillrumstranda beach, near Namsos. However, as the propeller tips were damaged the Skua could not take off again so the Skua was blown up on April 1st by British forces to prevent it falling into enemy hands.

Above: Skua L3049 'L' served with 800 Squadron in the Mediterranean, where the squadron operated from Ark Royal from July 1940 to April 1941. The colour scheme was revised at this time with the lower surface colour changing from sky grey to the 'duck egg' greenish sky. Type A1 roundels were applied to the fuselage and full fin-flashes worn. Single aircraft letters moved from the fin to the fuselage and were white-outlined black.
Below: The first production Roc was L3057 and as there were no prototypes, this aircraft was used mainly for development. It first flew on the 23rd December 1938 and was used for a range of tests including handling, performance and the floatplane modification 'kit'.

Blackburn Skua & Roc

153

L3059 was the third production Roc and its short career was all spent on the development programme. The aircraft was used for comparative trials with L3057 on different propellers, and was then converted to floatplane configuration at the Marine Aeroplane Evaluation Establishment, Helensburgh. The floats were found to affect handling, and L3059 crashed on the 3rd December 1939 and was written off.

Above: This unidentified Roc was photographed at Eastleigh in late 1939 or early 1940, and appears to be in an all-over black colour scheme in common with several other aircraft including Skuas and Gladiators, but retaining Type A roundels on fuselage and wing undersides. The reason for the colour scheme is unknown.

Below: Roc L3084 was captured in a pre-war photo-shoot. The first Rocs left the factory in the same all-over silver scheme as all Skuas, though most were camouflaged by Boulton Paul where they were built. L3084 displayed some variations on the standard silver scheme with Type A1 fuselage roundels instead of type A, and an unusual full-height, narrow chord fin flash.

Blackburn Skua & Roc

155

Above: Roc L3085 was camouflaged in the standard Royal Navy temperate sea scheme, but was actually operated by the RAF in the Air-Sea Rescue role. The Roc was the personal aircraft of Pilot-Officer D.H. Clarke, who decorated it with the 'Saint' logo on the rear fuselage. The aircraft was written-off following a battle with a Heinkel He59 which was claimed as damaged on September 26th 1940.
Below: Roc L3086 was one of several that were used in the target tug role at Dekheila in Egypt (L3154 was another). These Rocs were modified simply by removing the turrets and attaching target towing gear. Photographs suggest they were very well used as they show considerable wear, repainting and patching, and a range of colour schemes.

Above: L3105 was a Roc assigned to 806 Squadron and as such probably saw action over the beaches of Dunkirk. The squadron undertook fighter patrols and dive bombing with Skuas and Rocs until relieved by 801 Squadron at the end of May 1940. As the squadrons applied their own markings, each had a slightly different interpretation in colours, location of demarcation between upper and lower camouflage, codes and serials.
Bottom: Roc L3100 served in the target tug role, ending up with 773 Fleet Requirement Unit in Bermuda in 1943. The colour scheme is unusual, with the upper surface colours extended down the sides of the fuselage for its entire length, but the fin and rudder left sky or sky grey as with the earlier RN schemes.

Blackburn Skua & Roc

157

Blackburn Skua & Roc

Above: L3147 was the subject of a photoshoot in 1941 which showed the aircraft in excellent detail. It was evidently used by the RAF for training or Anti-Aircraft Co-operation, despite its modified Fleet Air Arm camouflage, as it the pilot was a Flight Lieutenant Thompson.
Below: In February 1940, the RN proposed gifting 33 Rocs to Finland, which was using a wide variety of more-or-less obsolete machinery against the Soviet Union. The Rocs were gathered at Dyce where they had Finnish serials applied and roundels covered with white discs. Some photographs show what appears to be Finnish 'swastikas' roughly overpainted, possibly with temporary distemper, to disguise their destination during transit. The 'Winter War' ended before the Rocs could be delivered so they reverted to British ownership.

A rare colour postcard of a Skua in pre-war silver flying over a destroyer and the carrier Ark Royal. As with much Skua artwork, the picture evokes speed and power, somewhat at odds with the reality.

A pre-war postcard of a Skua diving. The colours are similar to those worn by Ark Royal's squadrons in 1939 though they have possibly been interpreted from a black and white photograph - the tail bands are similar to those shown on contemporary photographs of L2887, which may have been mistakenly rendered as L2882 by the artist. The caption erroneously states that power was from a Bristol Pegasus rather than Perseus.

Recent kits of the Skua and Roc from Special Hobby in 1/48 scale and with injection-moulded, resin and etched brass components.

Blackburn Skua Mk.II, Cat. # SH48046 in 1/48.

Blackburn Roc, Cat. # SH48050, in 1/48.